What people are

God-Inspired

"This thought provoking book encourages us to reflect on our unique precious life and how we can grow into God's inspired potential for each one of us. Godfrey Kesari's book is well earthed in Scripture and personal experience of ministry in India and the U.K. Suitable for group reflection, it could also be the basis for personal devotion and retreat."
Revd Ernie Whalley, President of the Baptist Union of Great Britain 2013–2014

"Our society urgently needs Christians who are true disciples of Christ, men and women who have living relationship with God through Jesus. He came 'that we might have life, and have it to the full.' Godfrey Kesari invites us to accept the challenge to live through love and light each day in the presence of God. This book offers us practical advice on how to set out on that journey."
Revd Provost Anthony Churchill S.T.L. Episcopal Vicar for Ecumenical Affairs, Roman Catholic Diocese of Arundel and Brighton, UK

"This book contains anecdotes, stories and examples that profoundly help to lead its readers closer to God. Godfrey Kesari succinctly points to the challenges each of us face in life and provides direction in restoring a right relationship with God and with each other, challenging us to live differently. I highly recommend this book for everyone who aspires to a God-inspired life and witness in this world."
Revd Dr Solomon Sudhakar, Ordained Minister serving the Northern Illinois Conference of the United Methodist Church, USA

"To read Godfrey Kesari's *God-Inspired Life: Living Differently Through the Six Challenges of Life* is to read accessible systematic/pastoral theology that is food for the Christian soul. Godfrey's awareness of the challenges that humans face, in their relationships, and in regard to purpose, and his ability to communicate that God is the God who guides and inspires us at those times, is extremely rich. I hope to utilize this book with my congregation—with a group of thoughtful adults who want to understand how to apply doctrine to the realities of human existence."

Revd Seth Kaper-Dale, Co-pastor of the Reformed Church of Highland Park, NJ, USA

God-Inspired Life

Living Differently Through the Six Challenges of Life

God-Inspired Life

Living Differently Through the Six Challenges of Life

Godfrey Kesari

CIRCLE
BOOKS

Winchester, UK
Washington, USA

JOHN HUNT PUBLISHING

First published by Circle Books, 2022
Circle Books is an imprint of John Hunt Publishing Ltd., No. 3 East St., Alresford,
Hampshire SO24 9EE, UK
office@jhpbooks.com
www.johnhuntpublishing.com
www.circle-books.com

For distributor details and how to order please visit the 'Ordering' section on our website.

ISBN: 978 1 78535 943 9
978 1 78535 944 6 (ebook)
Library of Congress Control Number: 2021942801

A CIP catalogue record for this book is available from the British Library.

Design: Matthew Greenfield

UK: Printed and bound by CPI Group (UK) Ltd, Croydon, CR0 4YY
US: Printed and bound by Thomson Shore, 7300 West Joy Road, Dexter, MI 48130

We operate a distinctive and ethical publishing philosophy in
all areas of our business, from our global network of authors to
production and worldwide distribution.

Contents

Acknowledgments

I thank God, first and foremost, for His guidance, grace and love which I needed and relied on from the beginning until the conclusion of this work. I couldn't have done this without the constant assertion that it is He who used me to work on this guidebook.

Many people kindly helped in the formation of this book. G David Milton, one of my cousins, read through the initial manuscript and offered his encouragement together with invaluable suggestions. My sincere thanks go to him. I also wish to thank Aldin Philo, one of my nephews, for the many car journeys accompanying me to meet with my cousin. I will cherish the good times we had together. My gratitude extends to other faithful believers who read parts of the original manuscript and offered their constructive comments. To mention them here – Daphne Ford and Anthony Halford of the Priory Church of St Mary, Bridlington, Yorkshire; Simon Kirby of St George's Church, Edgbaston, Birmingham; Pat Chapman, Julia Handley, Debbie Moore and Paul and Alison Hudson of the Holy Innocents Church, Southwater, West Sussex. I want to acknowledge and thank them for their candid remarks and support. I am also enormously grateful to the Home Group of Southwater Parish Church for their benevolence in giving me their reassurance, which kept me going all along.

This book contains anecdotes, stories and incidents or more precisely recollections of them shared with me by pastors, family members and friends. As a parish priest I have listened to countless sermons and presentations in different churches too. I want to acknowledge that I am just passing on the knowledge I gained over many years in a structured way in this book. Thanks a lot to everyone, who has molded my life with their care and love either directly or indirectly. My intention in writing this book is that it will bring readers much closer to God, His light, joy and love. My prayer is that it will help them live differently, with hope, for greater and better things. We are never alone as we seek to live for God in Christ because He is always with us. To God be the glory forever.

I am deeply indebted to the editors and all the staff at Circle Books, John Hunt Publishing, for their wonderful support and help in publishing this book.

Finally, my grateful thanks go to my parents for their prayers. I also thank Pradhma, my wife, for her fervent support and our children Emy and Evans for cheerfully sharing the burden and blessings of the ministry, of which the writing of this book is a part.

As I continue to learn to live a God-inspired life every day, if this work can help bring clarity, insight, joy and transformation in the life of readers and promote holy and happy living, I would be delighted.

Declaration of Commitment

With the help of God, I intend to come closer to Him day by day.

With the help of God, I intend to bring clarity and focus into my life.

With the help of God, I intend to make decisions that will change my life for the better.

With the help of God, I intend to live the rest of my life for Him.

With the help of God, I intend to take the time to pray – listen to Him and talk with Him – if I am prompted while reading this book.

Signed by..

Your name..

Date..

I have already prayed for God's blessings on all who will read this book.

My commitment is to continue to pray for you.

Godfrey Kesari

Again, truly I tell you that if two of you on earth agree about anything they ask for, it will be done for them by my Father in heaven.
(Matthew 18.19 NIV)

Preface

Your own ears will hear him. Right behind you a voice will say,
"This is the way you should go," whether to the right or to the left.
(Isaiah 30.21 NLT)

Who inspires you? Is it yourself or is it somebody else? Do you
ask God and wait for Him to guide your life every day?

Many live an others-inspired life. If you constantly live a
life that is inspired by others you can become exhausted. The
truth is no one will have the approval of everyone all the time.
You do not have to prove yourself to anyone. You only need the
endorsement of God. If you live a life that God delights in, you
will be blessed. To give you one example, King Rehoboam loved
to have the approval of his young friends. He listened to them
and increased taxes. Understandably, people rebelled, and his
kingdom became divided. During the reign of King Solomon,
the father of King Rehoboam, God had anointed elders after
His own heart to give counsel to the king. Rehoboam did not
listen to them. He learned the hard way that he needed to obey
God and not be led by others. We are made by God to live a life
inspired by Him.

Many others live a self-inspired life. A self-inspired life can
be fun. You might be enjoying your life's journey at the moment
but one day if you realize that you've been heading in the wrong
direction all along it will be very disappointing for you. For
instance, if you decide to go to New York from London and if
you board a plane that goes to Sydney you might still enjoy the
journey. Nevertheless, once you realize that you are traveling in
the wrong direction you will have to make a U-turn. There was
a rich young man who came to Jesus. He asked Jesus, "What
must I do to inherit eternal life?" He kept the law and as far we
know he was happy. Jesus said, "Give your money to the poor

and follow me." Apparently, he was living a self-inspired life. He did not want to know where real riches and joy lie. He sadly left Jesus. God in Jesus lovingly wanted him to learn that it is not materialism or popularity that makes one really rich, but the knowledge of the presence of God in Christ with him. The good news is God in Christ, through His Holy Spirit, inspires, guides and leads us in the right direction when we wait on Him. A God-inspired life will be fulfilling not only now but also eternally.

Sometimes we can lack inspiration. Uninspired life can lead us to loss of vision, direction, focus and purpose in life. We need clarity, focus and meaning. We need God. This book, I believe, will be a guide to show how our life will look if we ask God to be our first priority of our lives.

A God-inspired life can reduce unrealistic expectations, confusions and lead to a holy way of life. An understanding of God's purposes for the six different challenges of our life will help us to be more content and peaceful.

The six challenges of our life, identified in this book are

(1) maintaining our relationship with God,
(2) maintaining our relationship with each other,
(3) understanding God's call,
(4) overcoming temptations,
(5) enduring suffering, and
(6) preparing for heaven.

If you want to see how a God-inspired life will look – look at Jesus. In the Bible, we read about Him living purposefully through the six challenges of life. First, look at His prayer life which was a top priority for Him even in his busiest days. Look at His trust in God, the Father through the Holy Spirit. Look at His knowledge of the scripture. Look at His regular worship life. Jesus' life teaches us that we need to relate to God every day. Second, look at Jesus' love and compassion. Look at His kindness towards humanity. Look at the time He spends building others. His life portrays that we as human beings need each other. Third, look at Jesus' clear understanding of his vocation. Look at His passion for doing the father's will alone. He teaches us that discernment of God's will for us is vital. Fourth, look at how Jesus overcame temptations. Look at His focus on the Kingdom of God. Overcoming temptations, with the help of God, is something we can learn from Him. We will need God's help to receive forgiveness and start afresh too when we fail. Fifth, look at how Jesus holds on to faith in God the Father even on Good Friday. Look at His confidence to commit His spirit into the hands of the Father. Jesus' life makes transparent the ways in which we can get through difficult times. Sixth, look at Jesus' resurrection life. Look at His hope in everlasting life with God the Father in heaven. That is how a God-inspired life will look – full of love, purpose, meaning, direction, peace and hope.

This book, I trust and pray, will inspire you to grow in your faith in God. I also pray that God will bless you to become more and more of the person He wants you to be.

Introduction

On a bright sunny day, we see no clouds between the sun and us. Regardless of the weather, God is shining upon us every day. Nonetheless, fears, worries, confusions, sins, guilt and selfish ambitions come like clouds between God and us. Just as the winds disperse the clouds, the Holy Spirit of God helps clear anything between God and us when we seek His help in prayer. When the path between God and us is clear, with no "clouds" in between, we can look to God to inspire us in His ways, day after day. We begin to live the life that God wants us to live.

An earnest waiter enjoys waiting patiently to serve. We are meant to enjoy waiting on God every day. Every morning I pray for the concerns the world faces, God's blessings upon the local parish, church community, family and friends. Then I also pray, "God, inspire me to live for you and walk in your ways every moment today." It gives the finest start to the day. I also go back to God in prayer for His guidance during the day.

Often in this world we can get confused about our purposes, passions, perceptions and priorities. There are so many ungodly distractions in this world. Life can become messy. Well, nothing can renew and revitalize your life more than re-dedicating it to God. Seeking God's help will guide you in the right direction. It will also bring the peace and light of God into your life. This book is a pointer towards what a God-led life will look like in our world today.

In the past, I have wasted my energy and resources on trivial and petty things which don't have any deep or lasting significance. I come across people who worry too much about failures which will soon pass. A God-inspired life is much more than our achievements or failures. It is to connect with God in prayer and with those around us in godly love. Certainly, the Covid-19 pandemic had made many of us think about God's purposes in the light of the different challenges we face in this broken world. My prayer is this book will help you see life the way God sees it and it will motivate you to live for God.

This book explores the six predominant challenges of life. God wants us to live differently through all six facets of life by

(1) maintaining our relationship with God,
(2) maintaining our relationship with each other,
(3) understanding God's call,
(4) overcoming temptations,
(5) enduring suffering, and
(6) preparing for heaven.

You might wonder as to how I concluded that these are the six challenges of life. The prayer that God in Jesus Himself taught us has these six points within it. *Our Father, who art in heaven, hallowed be thy name* These words draw us to the fact that it is all about God. More than anything else, we are made to be in relationship with the Holy God. The first chapter is dedicated to this theme. When we pray – *Thy kingdom come* – we commit not only to loving God but also to loving our neighbor and to maintaining right relationship with others around us. God's kingdom will not be complete without you and others. Maintaining relationship with others is the topic of the second chapter. Chapter Three focuses on the third point in the Lord's Prayer. *Thy will be done on earth as it is in heaven* – this prayer portrays the importance of discernment. *Give us this day our daily bread* It is God who provides for our daily needs to live for Him. We will then move on to learn how to seek forgiveness when needed and overcome temptations in Chapter Four – *Forgive us our trespasses, as we forgive those who trespass against us. And lead us not into temptation …* We face evil things in this broken and fallen world. Hence, Jesus teaches us to pray – *deliver us from evil.* With God's help, we can get through the struggles of this world.

This is *reaffirmed* in Chapter Five. *For thine is the kingdom, the power and the glory, for ever and ever. Amen* – We acknowledge that all good things belong to God. The good news is God through His love and mercy has offered us the invitation to share in His kingdom, power and glory eternally. Preparing for a life in the direct presence of God is addressed in the final chapter.

Further, I have heard and read thousands of sermons from many different preachers from my childhood until now. All messages, based on scripture, church's tradition and wider issues fitted into one of these six broad themes. Thus, I concluded that these are the six challenges of our life in this world. These six challenges, in turn, point us towards the six purposes of our life.

Our life is God-given. It is a treasure. The most joyful life is one led in the way God intends it to be lived. My hope is that this book will bring strength, confidence, clarity, transformation, joy, peace and inspiration to you. I pray that God in Christ will lift your spirits beyond your imagination as you read on. May God bless you and make you instruments of His glory as you turn the pages.

Chapter 1

Life Is a Rechargeable Gift — God-Inspired Life Requires Us to Be Connected with God

1.1 Created to live a God-inspired life

God-inspired life begins with emptying yourself fully. It also requires opening yourself to God fully.

When I was a teenager, and in my twenties too, I used to feel "so great" and "very important." Over the decades I have learned that it is little about me and all about God. I feel much humbler now. It may be unpalatable, yet it is true that, without God, you and I are not so "great" as we often think we are. No matter whether we exist or not, the sun will rise tomorrow and the days to come. The earth will rotate on its axis even if we get out of it. Without you and me the stars will shine, winds will blow, the rains will pour down, the fishes in the ocean will swim and the trees will blossom. You and I are not at the center of the universe. God is.

It is a lesson worth learning to make life worth living for God. Once we learn the reality of the might of the almighty and our own insignificance in the scheme of things, digest it and let it sink in, it is very liberating in spirit. It is affirming in life. It unshackles you to live a God-inspired life. It enables you to be and become what God created you for. It inspires you to walk in God's ways. We are created by God to live a God-led life. It is all about emptying yourself fully and refilling yourself with God fully. That might take time. You will have to do it again and again. And it is a lifelong work. Nevertheless, to live a God-inspired life we need to let go of our "selves" or more precisely of our egos. God invites us to let go of our confusions, burdens, guilt, sins, losses and worries too. He asks us to cast them unto Him. We need to let God in Christ come into the core of our lives.

God made you so that He can delight in you. God made you so that you can enjoy God despite your circumstances both in this world and the next.

God-inspired life brings joy to God

A big question most people have is the reason for us to be here. We, as human beings, create things we love and that will stay with us. Look at your living room – the chairs, the sofas, the fireplace and so on are all meant to bring joy in your life. Or look at your kitchen or your washroom – all appliances you see in the kitchen, also the washing machine and dryer in your home are there for a purpose. Most of the things we own are human made. Why do we make them? We make them so that they will become part of our life. We make them to be instruments in our hands. God made us to be instruments in His hands. Just as our creations make us happy when they serve their purpose, God will be happy when we, as His creation, serve His purposes. God created us to live a life led by Him. God smiles when we strive to live a God-inspired life. Nothing else will make us more content than living a life led by God because that's what we are made for.

Of course, we are not furniture or gadgets – far from it. We are human beings. No matter whether you believe we were made through evolution or creation, we were made by God for His purposes. We can fulfill God's purpose of living a life motivated by God only by being connected with Him and filled by Him. The only difference between God's creation and our creation is that we create everything from something else, but God created everything out of nothing. We are made by God so that God can delight in us.

This is not just Christian understanding. Leaders of all the major and popular religions teach their followers to find their renewed vision in God. They teach that we are made for God's eternal purposes. They teach that we are created to live a God-led life.

Children look for opportunities to bring joy in parents' lives. Little children tend to tell jokes and sometimes even act silly to make their parents smile. I have often noticed that grown-up children give surprise parties for their mothers and fathers on their big birthdays and on their big anniversaries to make them happy. It is a way of saying "thank you" to parents. Similarly, we as children of God need to bring joy to God. God, our heavenly parent delights in us when we bring joy to Him. Spending time with God, changing our lives to more godly ways and giving our time and talents to God, will make God happy. We will see more of how we can bring joy to God throughout this book. Here, let me be clear that just as a child's instinct is to make the mother and father beam, our instinct is to make God beam although we can suppress our natural instinct. Let us not be confused or get distracted by less important and trivial things.

I did not conjure up this idea nor do I claim patent to it. People of God throughout centuries have known the unique and special relationship between God and humanity. In the Bible we read of hundreds of people who lived a God-inspired life. Nothing seemed more important to them. Why? Without perplexity they knew and understood that God had made them to bring delight and glory to Him. And God delighted in them. Throughout centuries people of Christian faith went all over the world and risked their lives to proclaim the good news in word and deed. Why? They knew that God would delight in them. Ultimately, that's what mattered to them.

Bringing joy to God will bring peace in our lives too.

God-inspired life reveals God's glory

The heavens declare the glory of God; the skies proclaim the work of his hands. Day after day they pour forth speech; night after night they reveal knowledge. They have no speech, they use no words; no sound is heard from them. Yet their voice goes out into all the earth,

their words to the ends of the world. In the heavens God has pitched
a tent for the sun. It is like a bridegroom coming out of his chamber,
like a champion rejoicing to run his course. It rises at one end of
the heavens and makes its circuit to the other; nothing is deprived
of its warmth.[1]

We are created to reveal God's glory too. Just as a polished
surface is capable of reflecting light, we are capable of reflecting
God's glory.

The trees, the animals, the birds, the sun, the moon, the stars
[and the galaxies] – are all there for a purpose, says the psalmist.
Creation reveals God's glory. We too reveal God's glory because
we are made in God's image. Perhaps the easiest place to look at
God's glory is in the mirror. There is God's glory on you. "You
and I are wonderfully and fearfully made."[2] Even when we don't
feel like it, we are special in God's eyes.

I guess many people question the purpose of God's creation
when they are confused, worried or feel unwanted. That is why
we need to be clear on what we are made for. This will help us
not only on good days but also on not-so-good days. God created
you and me not to ignore us or leave us confused or worried but
to be led by Him every day. In supermarkets we see products
made by different companies. We also often see the brand name
on the product. The brand name on us is God's glory. When we
look at ourselves and at each other, we need to open our eyes to
see God's light and image.

It is normal and natural to question the reason why God has
put us on this planet. Many people secretly wish they had the
answer to this question. Our brains are wired in a way that now
and then we seek to find the reason for our existence in this
world. So, even if life is good for you at the moment, you might
be living with this question. This book assumes that we are
created to live a God-inspired life. But how? To live a God-led
life is to be channels of God's glory. As long as we are connected

with God or soaked in God, and what we do with our life reveals God's glory, God will be pleased with us.

Not all are called to channel God's glory in the same way, but everyone is called to show forth God's glory by living for God, for God's people and for themselves. It brings immense pleasure to God when we reveal His glory by living life in godly ways – giving thanks to God every day.

The truth is God's glory fully dwelt in Jesus.[3] God's splendor disclosed in all that Jesus said and did. Despite our foibles, fallibilities and fragilities we too can glorify God. The psalmist pleads, "Let me live so I can praise you."[4] He sees the purpose of life is to praise God. All we need to do is God-glorification and not self-glorification. There is a relief in knowing that God-guided life is not to bring glory to ourselves, which doesn't have lasting significance, but to bring glory to God, which has eternal significance.

Nonetheless, it is impossible to live a life that brings joy and glory to God by our strength alone. We need to ask God to help us. Please read this prayer before we move on: "Loving God, heavenly Jesus – I do want to bring joy to you, I do want to reflect your glory. I pray for your help and inspiration. Bless me and use me through your Holy Spirit for the purposes you have made me. Grant me all blessings and grace I need to live a life filled and guided by you and you alone. In Jesus' name. Amen."

God-inspired life is to receive what God offers

Remain in me, as I also remain in you. No branch can bear fruit by itself; it must remain in the vine. Neither can you bear fruit unless you remain in me. I am the vine; you are the branches. If you remain in me and I in you, you will bear much fruit; apart from me you can do nothing.[5]

Again Jesus said, "Peace be with you! As the Father has sent me,

I am sending you." And with that he breathed on them and said, "Receive the Holy Spirit."[6]

We are created to receive what God has to offer – again and again. God not only created us but also has given us the wisdom, strength, peace, grace and most importantly the Holy Spirit to live a God-inspired life. The fact is we breathe because God wants us to live. It is by God's grace alone we can be what God would like us to be with our life. And God is not tight-fisted. The more we receive from God the more God is ready to offer.

Often, we get confused and give up because we try to live on our own strength. Our resources are limited. We can get "burnt out" easily. We need to acknowledge that we have the Holy Spirit in us. We can also receive the Holy Spirit in a fresh way when we ask God for it in prayer. All gifts of life come from God and God provides all the resources we need, in His time, to live life in its fullness, in His eyes.

God gives the Holy Spirit in a fresh way to those who ask for that gift. When we ask for the gift of the Spirit, we must believe that we have received the gift. The Holy Spirit of God helps us to fulfill plainly God's purpose for our life. Just as a car cannot keep on fulfilling its purpose without going to the garage to get fuel, we cannot keep on fulfilling our purpose in life without coming to God again and again to receive God's spirit within us.

God also provides peace and confidence in our hearts to be and to become who we really are. All we have to do is to leave our hearts, hands and lives open so that God's light is drawn in. God is astonishingly generous, and He gives us the gifts we need when we pray. Our task is to take time to open our hearts to receive God's holy gifts.

Remember, we don't have to use a gift which God has not given us, which might come as a relief to us. The truth is God has given everyone gifts. In a parish I served previously, I used to visit a lady who was bed-ridden for 12 years. She couldn't even move on her bed. She always told me, "My gift is to pray. I will pray for you." I always felt blessed when I visited her. I sensed God's presence with her every time I was there. What are the gifts God has given you? Prior to doing anything, we need to pause to receive. Take time to receive what God has to offer – joy, glory and His Spirit.

St. Paul talks about the different gifts God gives to different people. No one has all the gifts, and no one is without any gifts. We are to acknowledge our God-given gifts with gratitude. We are to pause to receive God's blessing for us that day.

Questions for reflection or discussion

1. In what ways could you bring joy to God who created you?
2. What do you understand by the word glory?
3. How would you describe the "glorious moments" in your life?
4. Do you think there is something special about you and all others around you?
5. Do you think a God-inspired life will bring more clarity to your life?
6. "Receive the Holy Spirit," said Jesus. Why don't you take a moment to ask for that gift? If you are in a group, you could take a moment to pray silently for others and yourself.

1.2 God inspired life is to know God, love God and to be in relationship with God

As we saw earlier, we are created to receive the most precious gift – that is God himself through His Spirit, whom we need to receive again and again. Similarly, we are made by God to get to know God more and more every day. After all, we are going to spend our entire life with God in this world and our permanent life in God's direct presence.

Many people believe in God but live a self-filled life. This is because they are not sure how to live a God-filled life. God is always willing to guide our lives in His ways to live a God-inspired life. But first we need to get to know God, love God and be in right relationship with God.

Knowing about God and knowing God

Thus says the Lord: Do not let the wise boast in their wisdom, do not let the mighty boast in their might, do not let the wealthy boast in their wealth; but let those who boast – boast in this, that they understand and know me, that I am the Lord.[7]

Knowing about God is as important as knowing God because very often knowing about God precedes knowing God. However, knowing about God is quite different from knowing God. We can know about God by attending Sunday school, youth groups and worship services at the local church. We can also know about God by reading the Bible and many other good books about God. A good friend who believes in God can also share with us things about God. Listening to Christian hymns and songs or singing them can also give us a good understanding about God.

Nevertheless, to know God we need to take time in our otherwise busy lives just to be with God. We need to make this a godly habit. And one day we are sure to find Him because God promises that those who seek Him will find him. God keeps His promises. The Bible has this to say. "From there you will seek the LORD your God, and you will find him if you search after him with all your heart and soul."[8]

My fervent hope and prayer is that you will find God soon if you don't believe in God yet. Faith is more often caught than taught. If you are a believer already, my hope is that this book will reaffirm your faith. Also, it will help you grow stronger in your faith in God.

Knowing God is a matter of having a right and humble attitude before God. Also, it is not a one-time matter. It is a process. The more time we spend with God talking with Him and listening to Him, the more we get to know God. There is a tremendous joy in getting to know God as we get to know a good and faithful friend. That knowing God will guide our life in God's ways cannot be over emphasized.

There is a thought-provoking story about three prospectors who found a rich vein of gold in California during the gold rush days. They realized what a great discovery they had, and decided, "We've a really good thing going here as long as no one else finds out about it." So, they each took a vow to keep it secret. But people found out very quickly what had happened. The give-away was the expression on their faces. They were aglow in anticipation of the wealth that soon would be theirs. People knew that they must have found something very special. So, a crowd followed them out of town.

Knowing God is a joy like no other. It will change our life for the better.

God-inspired life is to love God with everything we have

Matthew writes, *and one of them, a lawyer, asked [Jesus] a question to test him, "Teacher, which commandment in the law is the greatest?" He said to him, "You shall love the Lord your God with all your heart, and with all your soul, and with all your mind. This is the greatest and first commandment."*[9]

With all your heart. Loving God with all our heart is to put our trust in God and give God our heart. If you or I need heart surgery we rely completely on the surgeon, giving ourselves into his or her hands. Similarly, loving God with all our heart is to offer our heart to God in trust so that God can do "spiritual surgery" in us and grant us a new heart. If Christian Bernard could give a "new physical heart" by means of transplantation, Jesus would certainly give a "new spiritual heart" by means of the love demonstrated on the cross.

With all your mind. Giving our attention to God prior to everything we say and do is to love God with all our mind. It is allowing God be part of all that we think. The inclusion of God in our thinking process is sure to reflect in what we say and do and make us into better and freer human beings.

With all your soul. The Greek root word for soul is psyche. We get the word – psychology from this root word. In Greek philosophy it meant with all that you have in your innermost being. (Life breath – is another translation.) This is an invitation to offer the deepest part of you to God in love and worship. Indeed, we become our authentic selves when we offer our souls to God.

With all your strength. This is to love God with all our physical, emotional, relational, and spiritual strength. Without love we cannot please God. Thankfully, Jesus clarifies our first purpose in life – which is to love God with everything we have.

God-inspired life is to build a relationship with God

For I am convinced that neither death nor life, neither angels nor demons, neither the present nor the future, nor any powers, neither height nor depth, nor anything else in creation, will be able to separate us from the love of God that is in Christ Jesus our Lord.[10]

Our relationship with God needs to be stronger than life or death. Paul is convinced that nothing can separate him [God's people] from the love of God in Christ.

Now, how do we establish a relationship with God? It is a two-way process. God calls you and me by name. God called

Moses, Abraham, Samuel, Deborah, Gideon, Isaiah, Mary, and you by name. Why? Calling by name meant that you are interested in them. It meant that you want personal ties to be established with them. In Jewish culture, it meant that you want to connect with them.

God calls you and me by our names. But how do we know this? One definition of God is love. Love calls His children by name. We are God's children. You hear God calling you by name when you listen in faith.

When God called Moses by name this is what happened. He was taken to another belief system. That, of course, is what encounters with God do. It happened not just to Moses but to everyone, mentioned in the scripture, who wanted to build a relationship with God.

Moses encountered God and he spent time with God near a burning bush. God said, "I am who I am." It's a verb and not a noun. Implicit in this is that God is active. A new relationship began and the purpose of life for Moses was clarified. He was re-affirmed. The direction of his life was illuminated. More importantly, his attitude changed. He realized that with God's help life changes.

Interestingly, Moses realized the Holiness of God. God told Moses – the place you stand is holy. He was asked to remove his footwear and he did. The place we encounter God is holy. In rural churches in the east, even today, people wouldn't wear sandals inside the church. In Indian culture – removing sandals could mean that we have reached home – or "feel at home" is the message. Perhaps God is saying, "feel at home" with me.

Obviously, I write about Moses only to give an example. There are millions and millions of other people throughout the centuries who made themselves at home with God. God invites everyone, including you, to feel at home with him. In other words, God says, "be in relationship with me."

Our names flow from God's lips naturally. He calls Moses,

17

Mary and each one of us by name. We are to know God's name and use God's name often. The name for God in the Old Testament is Yahweh. The Israelites did not use God's name out of respect. In the East, even today, people don't use the name of people older than them. There are different words for older brother, older sister and so on. In the West, we don't call parents or grandparents by their names either. However, we know, through the New Testament that God came to us in Jesus. So, we can use God's name in praise, prayer and thanksgiving. God wanted us to know God's name so that we could have a close relationship with God. Worship is about relationship. We renew and refresh our relationship with God through worship. We shall see more about worship later in this book.

Significantly, our connection with God leads us to a new beginning. It is about our transformation, transfiguration, direction and purpose.

My prayer is that God will give you the freedom and courage to hear him call you by name as well as the eagerness and confidence in your heart to be in relationship with God. Establishing and building our relationship with God is a prime purpose of our life. It is a life-long process. Heaven is about being in a relationship with God in God's direct presence. Why don't we begin to practice it now?

This is crucial because our relationship with God is what shapes what we do in life. To put it differently, when we are in the right relationship with God, we will have inner peace in our hearts.

Questions for reflection or discussion

1. Without knowing God it is difficult to have a clear idea of our purpose in life. What are some of the things we can do to know God better?
2. How can we grow in our love for God? Give practical examples if you can.

3. Do you prefer to know God by "faith seeking understanding" or "understanding seeking faith"? And why?
4. Paul is convinced that nothing can separate him from the love of God that is in Christ Jesus. What are the common things that separate people from the love of God? How can we overcome them?
5. What do you understand by the word, relationship? How is our relationship with God similar to our relationship with friends? How is it different?
6. Relationship with God is about new beginnings. How would you like new beginnings in your life?

1.3 Find your belonging, security, value and peace in God

Know that the LORD, he is God! It is he, who made us, and we are his; we are his people, and the sheep of his pasture.[11]

Having looked at the significance of being in right relationship with God, we now delve into the importance of finding our belonging, security, value and peace in God.

We all know that we need to have our basic needs met just to survive. We all need food to eat, water to drink, air to breathe, shelter to protect and clothes to wear. Modern day activists add education, sanitation and health care to the basic needs list. However, we often overlook the fact that we also need a sense of belonging, security, value and peace. Often, people struggle with confusion when there is no sense of belonging, security, value or peace.

Understandably, we are people who become easily worried. Children feel a great need to be loved in their childhood and nothing saddens them more than the lack of affection from parents and family members. At school some worry about grades, others worry about being too popular and yet others worry about not being popular. We grow up before we know it. We worry about the pressure of work and job security. We worry about missing out on things. And as we get older health problems become more frequent. So, worry can be part of all stages in life. However, God in Christ says that we need not worry but instead put our trust in God. To live a God-inspired life is to find our belonging, security, value and peace at all stages of life, in Him.

We belong to God now and eternally

I used to visit an orphanage in India. I have to say that many orphans sadly struggle to develop a sense of belonging. They have to work harder to come to terms with questions like Who am I? Whom do I belong to? Where can I find my security and value? And with whom can I find peace?

In a deeper sense, we all have these questions. Some scientists, who don't believe in the existence of God, would say that we are made from particles (stardust) of the universe. We belong to the natural cycle of things which means that when we die, we might become part of the grass that grows in the graveyard. A deer might eat the grass and a tiger might eat the deer and so as years pass by, we will become part of something else in the universe. According to them that is it.

God invites us to believe that there is more, and we are much more special than that. The Bible clearly states that we belong to God. *But you belong to God, my dear children. You have already won a victory over those people, because the Spirit who lives in you is greater than the spirit who lives in the world.*[12] We can acknowledge to God every day that we belong to Him. That will mean that our achievements belong to God and our worries and fears belong to God too. And God will help us to deal with them.

In fact, we can have a multiple sense of belonging. Children might think that they belong to their school or college. We might say that we belong to our family. We might belong to different clubs too. We might think we belong to our Church. People also say that they belong to a village, town or city. It is perfectly understandable that people have these multiple senses of belonging.

If we don't have a sense of belonging to friends, family, colleagues, community and church we might eventually lose interest in life itself. However, ultimately the point is God wants us to know that we belong to Him now and eternally. We are His beloved children. Every day we need to take time to build this sense of belonging to God.

The Bible says, "But now, O Jacob, listen to the LORD who created you. O Israel, the one who formed you says, 'Do not be afraid, for I have ransomed you. I have called you by name; you are mine.'"[13] Further, the Psalmist sings, *The earth is the Lord's and all that is in it, the world, and those who live in it.*[14] This is a verse to hold to heart and remember. When we feel "low" or when we lose a sense of belonging, we can take enormous comfort from the fact that we belong to God.

It is because we belong to God the only right way to live is to live for God. In other words, our purpose should be to live for God in Christ. Of course, this doesn't mean that everyone should become a priest or a pastor, but it does mean that we need to please God in all that we are in life. Once Jesus was asked whether it was lawful to pay taxes or not. Jesus asked them to show him a coin. As you might know, in the story, the coin had Caesar's image on it. Jesus said, "give to Caesar what belongs to Caesar and give to God what belongs to God."[15] In those days, there were the temple coins in use alongside the state coins and so Jesus' reply was poignant. Nonetheless, Jesus was also saying that you and I need to give God what belongs to God. We are made in God's image – and thereby we belong to God.

Thankfully, we belong to God not only now but also eternally. To those who have chosen to walk with God in Christ,

Max Lucado writes, "You'll be home soon. You may not have noticed it, but you are closer to home than ever before. Each moment is a step taken. Each breath is a page turned. Each day is a mile marked; a mountain climbed. You are closer to home than you've ever been, before you know it, your appointed arrival time will come; you'll descend the ramp and enter the City. You'll see faces that are waiting for you. You'll hear your name spoken by those who love you. And, maybe, just maybe – in the back, behind the crowds – the One who would rather die than live without you will remove his pierced hands from his heavenly robe ... and applaud."[16]

Belonging to God – Twice. There is a popular story of an eight-year-old boy who made a boat. He created it with wood, plastic, wax and other things. He painted it and it looked beautiful. He wrote his name inside it. He played with it on a river for many days. He rejoiced in his wonderful creation. His boat was his best mate and he loved his boat so much. After all it was his beautiful boat.

Unfortunately, one day while he was playing with his boat in the river there was sudden flooding and the rushing waters took his boat with it. As you would expect, the boy was extremely disappointed and sad. His parents consoled him and after a few days took him to a toyshop in the town. To his delight, he saw his own boat there. The shopkeeper had picked it up from the river. His parents wanted him to buy a better boat. The boy said, "No thank you, I will buy my boat with my pocket money." He asked, "How much is that boat?" – pointing his finger to the boat he made. He bought the boat and paid for it. The story says that later the boy told the boat, "You are mine not only because I made you but also because I have bought you. You belong to me – twice over."

God in Christ not only created us but also bought us for Himself by giving Himself up on the cross. Such is His love for us. We belong to God not only because He made us but also because He has redeemed us through His death on the cross and His glorious resurrection.

Many years ago, a lady who was feeling low asked me, "What should I live for?" She didn't have a family; she had lost interest in life and sadly I didn't know what to say. I am sorry to say that after a few days she took her own life. However, eventually I learned that we belong to God and the implication of that as our purpose in life should be to live for God. Reflecting on it later, I think I should have told her, "Live for Jesus, that's what matters." Perhaps the correct question to ask is, "Whom do I live for?" We belong not to ourselves but to God.

Security and value come from God

We not only belong to God, but our security and value comes from God too. Life in this world and life in our physical body is comparable to living in a rented house. Of course, the tenant has the responsibility to keep the house tidy and look after it. However, if there is a problem, it needs to be reported to the landlord. The ultimate security of the house is the landlord's responsibility. We too need to find our security in God who owns us.

The truth is that there are struggles in this world, but nothing can happen to you and me that God has not permitted. The Book of Job is clear in imparting this message. Actually, there are more than 80 verses in the Bible which say that God is our security. I shall quote two of them here.

"The eternal God is your refuge, and underneath are the everlasting arms."[17]

Jesus said, "I give them eternal life, and they shall never perish; no one will snatch them out of my hand."[18]

You and I are secure with God in this world and eternally. Nothing needs to stop us from living differently for God in Christ.

God's Value System

God's value system is apparent in the Sermon on the Mount.[19] Jesus' sermon was contrary to the economy of the world. He says, "Blessed are the poor." People did think that there must be something wrong about that message. But here Jesus has God's big picture in his mind. Jesus is saying that our value is not dependent on the material things we possess but it depends on the richness of God's spirit dwelling in us.

"Blessed are those who mourn for they will be comforted." God's value system is measured on whether we reach the hurt and share the burdens of others or not. "Blessed are the meek." Our value is based on whether we are controlled by others or God-controlled people. And then He says, "blessed are the pure in heart, for they will see God" – so deep, so profound – it makes you stop and think. Just as cataract surgery might help people see better, purity in heart helps people see God better. Our value is based on the purity of our heart. Blessed are the peace makers for they will be called the children of God. Nothing could be more valuable than being a child of God. Rejoice when you take risks for the gospel – your reward is great. God in Jesus invites his congregation to change their attitude towards life.

It is sad but you and I might not be precious in the eyes of the world. Not to worry, you are precious and valuable to God. Our purpose in life is to renew our attitude in the light of the Sermon on the Mount. Nothing is more lovable to God than you and I. You and I are so loved by God that Jesus died and rose again to forgive us and to re-connect us to God. As John's gospel puts it, the story doesn't end there. Jesus has gone to prepare a place for us[20] – the home where we all really belong.

Having lived in India for around 30 years and then moving to the UK, I used to feel terribly homesick. Whenever I visited India, I felt that was my home. However, after 18 years of life in the UK, when I visit India now, I don't feel the same way anymore. At present, I neither feel India is my home nor that the UK is my home. I very much doubt whether I would feel at home anywhere in this world anymore. No wonder Jesus whilst praying for his disciples says, "They are not of the world, just as I am not of the world."[21] If we want to live a God-led life we need to understand and accept that our home is in God. Also, we need to learn that our value is based on what Jesus has done for us on the cross and the peace of a holy life that God puts into our hearts and minds. We will see more about this in the following chapters.

God is our peace too

In the biblical sense, peace is not just absence of war. *Shalom*, the Hebrew word literally means an inner and outer well-being, completeness, wholeness, harmony and order. Peace is something inseparable from righteousness and justice. We need to keep the door of our heart open for God's peace to come in us. What we all long for is peace. We are wired to feel fulfilled and content when we are at peace. The source of our peace, light, enjoyment and pleasure is God. Corrie ten Boom famously said, "If you look at the world, you'll be distressed. If you look within, you'll be depressed. If you look up at God you'll be at rest."[22] The truth is that it is better to be in a "deep valley" with God than on a "mountain top" without God because with God there is everlasting peace and light.

St. Paul talks about the peace that passeth all understanding. For Paul, in spite of our circumstances, God's peace can dwell in our hearts. I have come across hundreds of people who testify to the peace they had even in very tragic situations in life. I have also come across an atheist who found God's light and peace at the funeral service of his own child. It might not have made sense, but he believed in God for the first time. It is all about opening our eyes – looking up to God – and asking for His peace. God pours His peace upon all who pray for it in good times and not so good times.

What has God in Christ to say about peace? Instead of

preaching a sermon, the risen Jesus himself came to his disciples, and said "peace be with you." Jesus knew that we need peace to live for God. Indeed, Christian faith affirms that Jesus died and rose again to re-establish our peace with God.

God invites us to know that we belong to God. To know that we belong to God is to know that we are secure in God and valued by God. The result is we receive the overflowing peace of God which this world cannot give in our hearts, minds and lives. It is very inspiring to find our true peace in and through God. In the next section, we will look at the meaning of the different names of God we read in the Bible which will enrich our life under God.

Questions for reflection or discussion

1. Do you think that a sense of belonging, security, value and peace are part of the basic emotional needs? If yes, in what ways?
2. We belong to God! Does that statement bother you or do you find it a comforting one?
3. What does it mean to say that in God we are secure? Do you think it is wise to find our security in God both now and eternally?
4. What are the differences between the value-system of the world and the value-system of God?
5. Where do you find your peace generally? Have you ever found God's peace in a difficult situation?
6. How would you interpret the phrase, "live for Jesus" to a friend?

1.4 Names of God-inspired life

God's names are glimpses of self-disclosure by God of His character and nature.

The names of God in the scripture are a "mirror-version" of exploring how to live a holy life. Just as looking at a mirror shows us our reflection, looking at the names of God can show us how God anticipates us to live. Rather than ignoring some names I shall put forward all of them briefly with the intention of understanding the relationship God intends to have with us. Names of God teach us God's will for our life too. To put it differently, we see who God is first and discern how God aims to help us live a God-inspired life.

The Triune God.

Christianity is a monotheistic religion although God has revealed Himself to humanity in three persons – Father, Son and Holy Spirit.

God, the Father. God revealed Himself as our father. Undoubtedly this tells us that God rejoices when we relate to Him just as children relate to their own father. Some children might not have a good father – so we need to bear in mind that God is a good father. A good father is always supportive to children. God, being the best heavenly father, is always supportive to us in our life.

God, the Son. The same God revealed Himself to us in Jesus so that God and His glory could become more intelligible to us. God also wanted us to know that, in Jesus, God understands humanity – our longings and needs. Our life is given to us and just as we keep in touch with our friends, Jesus wants us to relate to Him as a friend and a brother.

God, the Spirit. Indeed, we are also made for the Holy Spirit to abide in us. St. Augustine famously wrote, "Thou hast made us for Thyself, and our hearts are restless until they rest in Thee."[23] While Jesus lived in his physical body in this world, he was in one place at one time. Now we have the Holy Spirit who is always with us. This tells us that we are never alone. The spirit of God is God's gift to us to give us the assurance that the Spirit will guide us and lead us when we ask for it.

Names of God in the Old Testament and their implications for our life

Elohim (God) (Genesis 1.1) This is the very first name used for God. This name underpins God's majesty, splendor and omnipotence. *Elohim* is a plural word which implies that God is the most honorable and supreme being. This name suggests that our purpose of life is to give all honor to God. It also advocates that when we feel weak, we can ask God for strength and inspiration in prayer.

Yahweh (Lord, Jehovah) (Genesis 2.4) *Yahweh* is the promised proper name of God. It means Lord and Master. In Jewish tradition this name is too holy to pronounce. What is important to note is God is Lord and owner of all that He has created. This name reaffirms that God loves us, guides us and we belong to God.

El Elyon (The Most High God) (Genesis 14.18) This name of God says that God is the highest one. Our foremost purpose of life then is to worship God. We will see more about worship in the next section.

El Shaddai (Lord God Almighty) (Genesis 17.1) *El* is most likely linked to the word *Elohim* and is used in grouping with other eloquent words to specifically reference a particular characteristic of God. *Shaddai* derives from the word for a woman's breast (*shad*) and literally means "many breasted one." This denotes God as providing, supplying, nourishing, and satisfying His people with their needs as a mother would for her child. This name suggests that God is beyond gender and we need to thank God in prayer for sustaining us. Just as the love of a mother would enable a child to grow with confidence, the love of God enables us to grow in confidence in God.

El Olam (The Everlasting God) (Genesis 21.33) *Olam* means forever, always or unending future – in short, eternity. Used together *El Olam* means eternal God. God exists beyond time and space. We can take comfort in the fact that God always was, and always will be God. This name gives us the hope that we can live a God inspired life now and eternally.

Jehovah Jireh (The LORD Will Provide) (Genesis 22.14) God invites us to know that we are dependent on Him. This name is also an invitation to put our hope and trust in God who will provide.

Jehovah Rapha (The LORD Who Heals You) (Exodus 15.26) I am always fascinated to read the poster in my doctor's room (in India) which says, *We treat, God heals*. Healing is the nature of God; we can always go to God in prayer for healing in body or mind or spirit. Healing and inspiration often go together. God promises to be with us at all times.

Jehovah Nissi (The LORD Is My Banner) (Exodus 17.15) *Nissi* means flag or banner, so together *Jehovah Nissi* means the LORD Is My Banner. God himself is our banner and victory. God-inspired life is to give all glory to God as He is the one who wins our battles, in his time.

El Qanna (Jealous God) (Exodus 20.5) *Qanna* means jealous, zealous, or envy. Used together, *El Qanna* means Jealous God. God's jealousy is a holy one. No wonder, King Solomon writes, "The fear of the Lord is the beginning of wisdom."[24] This name is drawn from the marriage relationship with a picture of a husband jealous for his wife. God inspired life is to put God first in our lives, meaning in priority and substance because God knows what is truly best for us eternally.

Jehovah Mekoddishkem (The LORD Who Sanctifies You) (Exodus 31.13) *Mekoddishkem* means holy or set apart. It is the process of sanctification, which is the separation of something so that it is holy. Used together, Jehovah Mekoddishkem means that the Lord is the one who sanctifies you. God's intention is that we will ask God to sanctify us and make us holy because we are incapable of it on our own.

Jehovah Shalom (The LORD Is Peace) (Judges 6.24) *Shalom* means peace and wholeness. This name invites us to come to God when we are unable to deal with whatever problem is before us. God is the source of peace and we can find comfort and solace with God. **Jehovah Sabaoth (The LORD Of Hosts) (I Samuel 1.3)** *Sabaoth* means an army going out to war. Used together, *Jehovah Sabaoth* means the Lord of hosts or armies. God is always there to defend us, fight our battles, and win our wars. God sometimes allows us to go through difficulties, but nothing is there which cannot be defeated by God.

Jehovah Raah (The LORD Is My Shepherd) (Psalm 23.1) *Raah* means to shepherd or feed, to supply with food, and to be a good friend. Jehovah *Raah* means *The LORD Is My Shepherd*. God is a friend who provides overgenerous nourishment, protection, as well as rest for our weary bodies and souls. Just as a shepherd cares for the sheep, God cares for His people.

Jehovah Tsidkenu (The LORD Our Righteousness) (Jeremiah 23.6) *Tsidkenu* means justice, rightness, righteousness and deliverance. Our invitation thereby is to stay with God who provides us with His righteousness and justice when we don't have either in our lives.

Jehovah Shammah (The LORD Is There) (Ezekiel 48.35) *Shammah* is an adverb that simply means *there*, although when it's used in relation to time it means *then*. This name of God confirms that the Lord is there. We are invited to know that whatever we might be going through or whatever we might be about to go through, the Lord is already there.

Adonai (Master) (Genesis 15.2) Because the Jews have a tradition of not pronouncing nor spelling out the promised proper name of God, they often would use Adonai instead of YHWH. Adonai means *Lord*, *Master*, or *Owner*. This name emphasizes that God is in charge of His creation and His people, Lord of lords.

Names of God in the New Testament
I Am sayings of Jesus

I Am He (John 4. 1–26) A Samaritan woman asks Jesus about the Messiah. Jesus' response is I am He. We need to know Jesus is the Messiah and our salvation comes in and through God in Christ. In another place Jesus says, "I and the Father are one" (John 10.30). I can't emphasize enough that God – Father, Son and Holy Spirit is one and the same God.

I Am the Bread of Life (John 6. 25–51) Hunger hurts. Physical hunger as well as emotional and spiritual hunger hurts. Jesus not only provides food for our body but also for our soul. Whenever we are hungry, we can come to Him to be fed, renewed and refreshed. At Holy Communion services we hear the phrase, "Christ is the bread of life," which means Christ is the one who nourishes us.

I Am the Light (John 8. 12–30) Jesus is the light who sheds light on our path in life. It is wise to come to Him for light when there is darkness or little light in our path. It is wise to come to Him when we seek to live for God. We cannot search for anything in the dark. We can search for everything in life including the big question of meaning and purpose in the light of Jesus. Interestingly, God in Jesus is also the light within us. A Tamil theologian, who was blind, sang, *ul oli perukidavandum*, which means [God] increase the light inside of me. During gray and gloomy days, we do need God's light shining within us.

I Am the Good Shepherd (John 10. 1–21) Obviously, Jesus implies that He cares for us and loves us. In Palestine sheep were usually kept for wool rather than meat. The same sheep would stay with the same shepherd for many years. There is a close bond between the sheep and the shepherd. And the sheep even know the voice of the shepherd. Our life on this earth is to grow in that bond between God in Jesus and us.

I Am the Resurrection and the Life (John 11. 1–27) God in Jesus is our new life. Living differently is to know that God in Jesus can offer us new life whatever we might be going through. And ultimately this life is for our preparation for the life of resurrection at the end. We will devote more time to this in the final chapter.

I Am the Way, the Truth and The Life (John 14. 1–14) To say that Jesus is the way is to imitate Jesus. The more time we live in a foreign country the more we behave like the local people there. It might be quite uncomfortable in the beginning but we will get there. Similarly, the more time we spend in prayer and reading the word of God, the more we become like Jesus. The word truth implies that there are falsehoods in this world. God in Jesus affirms that He is the Truth and Life and we need to stick with Him.

I Am the True Vine (John 15.1–8) A branch disconnected from a plant is of no use. Within days the disconnected branches wither away. The apparent invitation here is to be connected with Jesus. A withered branch soon loses its identity and purpose. Our identity comes from our connectedness with God in Jesus, the True Vine. It is also essential to be connected with Jesus to live a fruitful life.

I Am the Alpha and Omega (Revelation 1. 8) Jesus here is saying that He is the beginning and the end. In other words, Jesus is everything. Our lives transform when we learn and understand that God in Jesus is whom we need. I know people who do two or three things in fear of missing out on matters in an evening. When we have God in Jesus, who is the Alpha and Omega with us we can be certain that we miss nothing.

Names of God reveal that God invites us to be connected with Him and to be dependent on Him. It is more about God and less about us. Taking time to go through the names of God can help us to understand God's nature better and thereby remember that God's help is at hand in all situations of our life. We need confidence to live a God-inspired life. Names of God can build and strengthen our confidence in God.

Having reflected briefly on the names of God, in the next sub-chapter we will move on to underpin the vitality of our worship life.

Questions for Reflection or Discussion

1. Do you think the concept of Trinity is important? Why do you think that God chose to reveal Himself to us as God the Father, God the Son and God the Holy Spirit?
2. How does learning the names of God help you?
3. Which names of God you think will stick with you and why?
4. Which characters of God come out again and again in the names of God?
5. How can the names of God help you build your confidence in God?
6. Do you prefer one of the "I Am" sayings to others? If yes or no, why?

1.5 God-inspired life is to worship Him

I was glad when they said to me, "Let us go to the house of the LORD." (Psalm 122.1 NLT)
God is spirit, and those who worship him must worship in spirit and truth.
(John 4.24 NRSV)

As we saw in the last sub-chapter, the names of God portray the love, beauty and holiness of God. Worshipping this matchless God in Christ regularly is at the heart of a God-inspired life. Whoever or whatever we worship is who or what will encourage us. God connects with us when we worship Him. But what is worship? The Hebrew word, *Shakah* – which is translated as worship – literally means to bow down. In saying, "O come let us worship and bow down; Let us kneel before the Lord, our Maker"[25] the Psalmist calls us to acknowledge that God is God and we are not.

The English word, *worship* – means attributing the ultimate worth to someone or something. Scripture, reason, religious traditions and spiritual experiences of many teach us that God alone is worthy of our imperative worship. We worship God in celebration of all that God has done, continues to do, and will do for us eternally. We worship the Lord in the beauty of His holiness.[26]

If we worship God in spirit and in truth, we cannot worship anyone or anything else. The truth is that everybody worships something. The need to worship is inherent in human makeup. The Bible puts forward that God alone is worthy of our worship. "Fear the LORD your God and serve him. Hold fast to him and take your oaths in his name."[27] Even if we go with logic, we can only worship God because there is nothing or no one greater than God. The Old Testament makes this call clear to us. "You shall have no other gods before me."[28] In the New Testament, Jesus Himself says, "It is written: 'Worship the Lord your God and serve him only.'"[29] The Book of Revelation claims that heaven is a place of worship.[30] God delights in us when we come to His presence in worship. The first mark of a God-inspired life is to worship God from the depth of our hearts in spirit and truth – not just out of duty, but also out of love for God.

What do we do when we worship?

We empty ourselves. We receive God's sprit, light and peace in us.

When we worship God, we actually empty our pride. We also empty our concerns and worries unto God. True worship is to bow down. Symbolically we say to God – all that is mine is actually yours. We empty ourselves and give all glory to God. Worship therefore includes praise and thanksgiving. We sing praises to God. Praise, honor and glory belong to God. When we praise God, we see ourselves in the right perspective. We become who we are. We give thanks for who God is, for all that we receive from God every day, for the assurance of our salvation and life eternal in and through the work of God in Christ.

We empty our concerns and burdens into the hands of Jesus because He has asked us to do so. During Jesus' time religion itself had become a burden. It is in that context Jesus says, "Come to me, all you who are weary and burdened, and I will give you rest."[31] Many think that taking time to worship God is another burden in our busy lives. In fact, worship is a time when we can offer our burdens – whatever they might be – to God. Also, taking time to worship God is a matter of joy. The heart of worship is encountering God who is the source of peace. It is a foretaste of heaven. It is communion with God – nothing can be more profound and joyful than that. Jesus himself went to the synagogue to worship God the Father, so it might be the right thing to do.

As we grow in worship, we also learn to repent and empty our sins before God. God cleanses us and absolves us of our sins and guilt. We also learn from scripture how to live a holy life and a life of truthfulness. In worship we affirm our faith and learn how to pray. And we are lifted up to God in prayer too. This prayer life is continued throughout our life.

In worship we evolve into who God intended us to be. We empty ourselves but we are also re-filled with God and by God. He fills us with His love, peace and hope. We are also strengthened by the faith and friendship of others in God's name. We are restored by transforming grace, replenished by the Spirit and re-assured of our salvation. Timothy Radcliffe in the final chapter of his book *Why go to church?* says that we go to church not only to worship but also to be sent out. In his words, "The slow working of grace will free me to be sent at the end."[32] We are sent into the world to live life Christianly, differently and purposefully.

Authentic worship

Authentic worship is something that comes from the heart. It is a transforming moment when you know that there is nothing – not even a tiny bit of fog – between you and God. Authentic worship is when our spiritual "inner" eyes are open, and we enjoy God's beauty, warmth and light. We really need God's help to worship Him authentically. It is always good to seek God's help for this in prayer as we prepare to worship.

God moments, as we worship, could be during singing or sermon or prayer or a moment of silence. Once you have those moments of God everything is transformed, you become a different person. It is hard to explain in words or prove to others but you will know that it is God and not a mere delusion when we encounter God in worship and prayer.

Authentic worship helps us re-focus. We all know that there are good things and bad things in this world. Authentic worship enables us to re-focus on good and godly things. Above all, authentic worship helps us to re-focus on God. That is to say, that the focus is not on music although music can lift us up to God. The focus is not on the craft of the sermon although it can be a pointer to God. Or the focus is not on eloquent prayers or our well-practiced performance throughout the service, but it is completely on God.

Worship is witness

Worship shows that we are dependent on God. I generally find people in England are good people. By and large people are interested in the welfare of others and do a lot of charity work too, thereby proving that they can be altruistic and not entirely selfish, as made out by noted evolutionary biologists. The NHS, the free education to children, heating allowances to the elderly and the social security system to the needy are all based on good Christian values.

One day as I was speaking with a person about life in general the visitor asked me, "Vicar, what do you want people to do?" Perhaps she expected me to say nothing; most people are already doing what they can. To her surprise my response was worship.

I would like people to worship regularly which will make it clear to ourselves that we actually rely upon God. It will edify our life and re-charge our spiritual batteries.

When we worship, we become witnesses too. In Western culture it is often hard to talk to people about faith. Many people love to talk about the weather but not God. However, when we come together to worship God it is a powerful witness to the community. Many churches live streamed worship services or made pre-recorded services for people during the recent pandemic. It was a useful thing to do. However, some worshippers expressed that coming together to worship is the real thing that has an uplifting feel to it. How we worship is not what really matters. What matters is that we worship God. When we gather together to worship God in church or via Zoom, we feel God's presence in a unique way. We also feel that we are there for each other in God's name.

Worship feeds us holistically

Worship and prayer enrich our lives. Many things we do in life make us poorer. I believe that the time we take to worship is what makes us rich in a higher sense. How? It is because worship time is relevant eternally. Worship is the language of heaven. If we are moving to a foreign country, wouldn't we want to learn the culture and language? I am persuaded that God will make every second of our worship and prayer time count eternally.

Worship is also a time we get fed by each other. The famous Alpha analogy of logs burning together well, whereas one log is easily put out, is relevant here. Worship is a time when we derive sustenance from God in Jesus, the bread of life.

Regular Worship

The fact is that everybody worships something. Some worship themselves and their own achievements while some others worship somebody else and their achievements. People can also worship their jobs, hobbies or even their own families. What comes first in our life is what we actually worship. A few years ago, I heard a headteacher at a local school ask a child to practice a reading "religiously." It made me think, as he had not permitted me to take assemblies at the school, even though I offered to take them. It made me realize that sometimes people do everything else "religiously" except worship God.

When we worship God regularly, we begin to see the bigger picture God has in His mind. This is important because when we know more of the way God looks at our life on earth our priorities change. We learn to put our time and energy in matters that God loves and that which makes us holy.

Regular worship at church or online inculcates the virtue of discipline in us. We are taught to practice what we believe and worship becomes something we do every day, not just on Sundays. The Bible asks us to offer our whole life as an offering of worship to God. In other words, our primary purpose of life is worship. As we will see in the final chapter, heaven is about worshipping God with all the angels, archangels and saints of God. When we worship God, we get a foretaste of heaven on earth.

Personally, I have made a commitment to God. I have committed to worship God at a local church whilst I am physically able and as long as I have the health to do so. When we hold on to God in worship and prayer when we can, God will hold on to us in grace and mercy when we can't.

Worship as the first priority

Worship is not one more thing we do in life. Worship shapes, informs, judges and transforms everything else we do. When we take time to worship God, God blesses the rest of our time in life. This means that God makes the rest of our time go further than it would have been otherwise.

The Olympic runner, whose life is celebrated in the movie

Chariots of Fire, Eric Liddell is a good example here. Eric Liddell was a committed Protestant Christian. Because the heats of the 100 meters sprint were held on Sunday, he withdrew from the race – a race considered to be his strongest. Instead, he concentrated on the 400 metres as the race schedule didn't involve a Sunday.

Liddell was considered to be a strong favorite for the race. Before the final, the US Olympic masseur slipped a piece of paper into his hand. It included the words from the Bible 1 Samuel 2:30 "Those who honour me I will honour."

Sprinting from the start, Liddell created a significant gap between him and the other runners and held on to win Gold and set a new Olympic record time of 47.6 seconds.

"The secret of my success over the 400m is that I run the first 200m as fast as I can. Then, for the second 200m, with God's help I run faster."[33]

We cannot live a God-inspired life if we do not commit to worship God. When we commit to worship God it is He that inspires our life, renews our every day so that we run extra spiritual miles during the time God gives us in this world to rejoice with Him, His people and His wider creation. Also, we should be careful to remember that Sunday worship is not a substitute for our everyday worship and prayer life.

God created us to relate with us. He loves when we enjoy His friendship. This is the prime purpose of our life. Having looked at the dimension of our relationship with God in this chapter, we will move on to explore our relationship with each other and the wider creation in the next chapter.

Questions for reflection or discussion

1. How important is worship for you? And why?
2. What do you think is the purpose of worship? Is it just a waste of time? Or what happens when people worship God?
3. Is prior preparation important for worship? If yes, how

can you prepare yourself?

4. Do you agree that worship is witness?

5. What are the differences between a non-worshipper and a worshipper?

6. Do you agree that worship has to be a priority for a Christian? And why?

Chapter 2

Life Is a Jigsaw Puzzle—
God-Inspired Life Is Mutuality

2.1 Cross human-made boundaries

We are spiritual beings having a human experience.
(Pierre Teilhard de Chardin)[1]

In the last chapter, we learned that we belong to God. The truth is we belong to each other too. God created us as social beings. Professor John Cacioppo of Chicago University is of the opinion that being acutely lonely is as stressful as being punched in the face by a stranger – and massively increases your risk of depression.[2] God created each of us in a unique way to belong to each other.

Of course, we are all made differently, and we all need our own space but at the core of being a human we are all similar. We share our humanity with others. We all come into this world, we all live and we all die. There is a commonality and oneness in our deepest being. In a deeper sense, when we look at others, we need to see God in them.

The scripture even teaches us that we need to make an effort to reconcile with our siblings before we can reconcile with God. Jesus says, "Therefore, if you are offering your gift at the altar and there remember that your brother has something against you, leave your gift there in front of the altar. First go and be reconciled to your brother, then come and offer your gift."[3]

Jesus began his ministry by saying to his first disciples Simon and Andrew, "Come, follow me ... I will make you fishers of men."[4] Thus, the kingdom of God is not a life in isolation but a life in relation with others.

Further, at the Lord's Supper, on the very day before Christ's death, he foretold his death on the cross and described it as sharing his body and blood. Gospel writers quote Christ's words, *This is my blood of the covenant, which is poured out for many.*[5]

Jesus is symbolized on the cross that we all share in the same body and blood. Hence, the eternal belonging to each other established on the cross, is not external but at the very heart of being a human.

Paul writes, "Make every effort to keep the unity of the Spirit through the bond of peace. There is one body and one Spirit, just as you were called to one hope when you were called; one Lord, one faith, one baptism; one God and Father of all, who is over all and through all and in all."[6]

We are not only members of the divine but also members of the common humanity so much so that to cause suffering and hurt to others is to do it to the divine. Our realization of this should encourage us to resolve conflicts, alleviate abject poverty and avoid profligacy waste. Such healthy teaching fosters essential values of health, beauty, compassion and empathy amongst humanity. Since we belong to each other we need to cross human-made boundaries of caste and race.

Casteism and Racism are unreasonable

Sadly, some in our world find ways to divide people. Some want to feel that they are superior to others. The problem of envy, comparing oneself with others, superiority complex and inferiority complex are as old as life itself. However, God-inspired life is not about comparing ourselves with others at all. The truth is God wants you to be you and not anybody else. No one can be you either. Life in this world is like a huge living jigsaw puzzle and everybody has a different but equally valued role to play. To live a God led life we need to know that all of us are unique and special. When we look at ourselves in the mirror and when we look at others' faces we need to see God in Christ living in us and in others. As Pierre Teilhard de Chardin says "We are spiritual beings having a human experience."[7]

It is unbelievable yet true, that even in this day and age in many villages, towns and cities in India and elsewhere, there is still the ignominy of the caste system. The centuries old problem of caste exists and divides people on the basis of the accident of birth. You can see that people of one caste do not interact with people of other castes. People do not enter the homes of people of a different caste. Caste is premised, based on the notions of purity and pollution and superiority and inferiority. Certain Hindu religious texts sanctify it. Hence, caste in India is sometimes described as "sanctified apartheid." The Dalits are at the "lowest rung" of the caste ladder. Nevertheless, I have seen children cross all boundaries of the caste system, playing and interacting with one another. No wonder Jesus said become like children. Jesus Himself, although a Jew, crossed boundaries to interact with the Samaritans and the Canaanites. We need to follow his model. He interacted with the Pharisees and Sadducees too and challenged them in the hope that they would turn back to God. This shows God's impartial and unchanging love for people of all shapes, sizes, color, nationalities and interests. His love surpasses all boundaries.

According to Paul, we all are given different gifts for the sake of unity. In his words, "So Christ himself gave the apostles, the prophets, the evangelists, the pastors and teachers to equip his people for works of service, so that the body of Christ may be built up until we all reach unity in the faith and in the knowledge of the Son of God and become mature, attaining to the whole measure of the fullness of Christ."[8]

To divide people based on caste is not only unreasonable but dehumanising too. This is because you don't choose your caste. You can't work hard and change your caste either. You are born into your caste and that is it. It is cruel that your caste is decided by others even before you are born. What logic is there in branding someone into a caste group if that individual did not choose it? What is the logic in upholding the caste system if we all are children of God?

Similarly, racism which is more recognizable universally is unreasonable because you don't have a choice to choose your features or color. What is the logic in discriminating against someone based on something that the individual did not choose or cannot change? The fact is there is only one race – the human race. The latest genetic studies establish that we are all the same under the skin. And real beauty is much deeper than the skin or its complexion. God looks at the heart and we must learn to do the same.

To live a God-inspired life is to commit to befriending one another and working for one another crossing all human-made boundaries of caste/ethnicity and race. We all are created as equal beings before God. Until we learn equality, respect for each other and mutuality we can't expect peace to prevail in this world. God created us to live cheek by jowl with others in communities and societies. While we all need our own space to live as individuals, we also need to know that we are one, in Christ, and God made us for each other.

Class divisions are unreasonable too

Unfortunately, often a human being's value is based on the material wealth one possesses rather than the very existence of a precious life. Life can be seen as a chess game. During the relatively short game the different pieces have different roles and powers. Nonetheless, when the game is over the King, the Queen and the Pawns go into the same box. That is true of life too. At the end of the day – despite our positions, powers, educational levels and bank balances – we all are equal before the eyes of God.

Jesus asked, "What will it profit a man if he gains the whole world, yet forfeits his soul? Or what can a man give in exchange for his soul?"[9]

One of the marks of a God-inspired life is to know deep within us that everyone is made in God's image and is equally valuable. God-inspired life is to do our bit without comparing ourselves with others. You and I are eternally precious and invaluable regardless of our worldly possessions and status.

The true import of this is fairer societies need to be created. Education opportunities must be provided to all, irrespective of their conditions. There needs to be free or affordable health services for everyone. Governments need to insist that developers must build affordable housing. Businesses need to be run not just to make profit but to serve as well. Structures in companies, industries, offices and churches should be seen as functional necessities rather than hierarchical powers. All this might be seen as humanly impossible, but this is what we need to aim for with the help of God. This is also the way we could bring a foretaste of God's kingdom into this world.

Love Crosses boundaries of Comfort Zones

A God-inspired life is not just to live for ourselves but for others too. It is well encapsulated in the second commandment which reads, *Love your neighbor as yourself.*[10]

Thus, Jesus teaches how relating ourselves to others is an essential part of a God-inspired life. We are created to love one another. This is possible only by inheriting God's loving nature in our hearts. We need to clothe ourselves with love.

I had a professor at theological college who often reminded us that the best thing for a pastor or priest to do is not to impress the congregation with their intelligence or to prove their leadership skills and great talents but simply to love the congregation with godly love.

This is true for people in any profession. A doctor or a nurse will do well when the patients know that they are loved and valued. A politician will thrive when people are listened to and cared for with love. A teacher will excel when students know that they are loved and so on. While Paul writes to Ephesians, amongst others[11] he makes it clear that he is writing to them neither for fame nor for money. There are many ways to look to win fame and accumulate money. Paul writes not because he doesn't have anything else to do either. He says that he writes to them because his love for them overflows. Whatever we do for ourselves and for others must be done in love.

The truth is there is so much pain in people who don't love. People sometimes talk about the pain of handicapped people and the pain of the poor. Having lived in the poorest parts of India I know very well that there is a huge amount of suffering in our world. However, the greatest suffering is in people who don't love and is in people who reject and neglect others. That is where we see how people can lock themselves up behind jails of comfort and security. It is a horrible prison because people lock themselves away from love, common humanity and compassion.

To live differently is to overcome our selfish desires and greed. It is to live not just to love ourselves, granted that is important, but to love others too. Love especially the ones in pain, the downtrodden and the needy. God is close to them and to us too if and when we feel low. We all know that a true friend is someone who stays with us even when we have lost our health or run out of money and resources. God created you and me to be a true friend to the needy and the suffering in the world. We need to trust that God is with us too when we struggle or face difficult times in life.

In fact, God and love are not two realities; they are one. God's being is the being of love. We are capable of giving and receiving love because God first loved us.

Sharing with the needy

There are plenty of biblical passages that invite us to love others. Sharing what we have with those who have none is a sign of

God-inspired life. God gives us food, water and resources to live. When we share part of what God has given us God blesses the rest of what we have. For Jesus, sharing with fellow beings is very much related to salvation. In Luke 19 we read about Zacchaeus. As soon as Zacchaeus says that he will share his possessions with others, Jesus replies that salvation has come to this house, because this man, too, is a son of Abraham, for the Son of Man came to seek and to save what was lost.[12] Sharing obviously is the product of our concern for others and thus directly portrays the human-human union aspect involved in it.

Jesus told the popular Good Samaritan story[13] to encourage us to look after one another in times of need. Moreover, Jesus makes it plain that whatever we do for the least is what we do for Jesus Himself.[14]

There is a story of someone who found a homeless man in terrible cold. He was so touched that he removed his coat and put it on that person. In the middle of the night the person who gave away his coat had a dream. He saw Jesus himself in his dream. To his pleasant surprise he saw Jesus wearing the same coat that he had given to the person in the cold.

Elsa Brändström is the daughter of a former Swedish ambassador to Russia. Seeing the horror of the First World War, she became a nurse. Paul Tillich writes this about her. "Love gave her wisdom with innocence, and a daring with foresight. She fed the hungry, she welcomed strangers, clothed the naked and strengthened the sick ... God was transparent in her every moment. It is a rare gift to meet a human being in whom love – and this means God – is so overwhelmingly manifest. It is the presence of God Himself, for God is love. And in every moment of genuine love, we are dwelling in God and God in us."[15] Love conquers everything.

Relating well with others will not only help us fulfill the purpose of human-human relationship for which we are created by God but will also make us truly beautiful. We will move on to explore this in the next sub-chapter.

Questions for reflection or discussion

1. Read Ephesians 4. 1–3 What are the qualities required to bring about unity and why?
2. Have your ever thought why we share peace before the offertory hymn?
3. What are common obstacles that prevent unity in our communities and society? How do we overcome them?
4. Read Ephesians 4. 11–13. What stands out for you in this passage? What is the central message?
5. What are the ways in which we can radiate the love of Christ in our church and community today?
6. Why do you think Paul calls the church the body of Christ?

2.2 God-inspired life is to become beautiful inside

The LORD does not look at the things people look at. People look at the outward appearance, but the LORD looks at the heart.[16]

People are like stained-glass windows. They sparkle and shine when the sun is out, but when the darkness sets in, their true beauty is revealed only if there is a light from within.
(Elisabeth Kübler-Ross)[17]

In the last sub-chapter, we looked at crossing boundaries. In this section, we will learn that a God-inspired life is not about becoming beautiful outside but inside. It is God's will that with His help we should transform and become beautiful inside just like a caterpillar transforms and becomes a butterfly.

Many people even at a younger age worry about getting older and their "good looks" fading away. Many do their best to help themselves look young and beautiful. We all look at the mirror and make sure that we look presentable when we go out. The bigger question to ask ourselves is if we would like to look beautiful before the eyes of God.

We will look at Stephen briefly, to learn how he made his face look beautiful like that of an angel. The Book of Acts tells us that the face of St. Stephen looked like the face of an angel. Precisely, Luke writes that Stephen's face shined like that of an angel.[18]

"Angelic faces" or "Faces shine like Angels'" could be a catchy phrase for advertising cosmetics or a beauty parlour. We see many people spending much money buying cosmetics and beauty products as well as spending considerable time in making themselves look beautiful and glamorous. Think about the cinema industry and how many millions of pounds go into the makeup products for actors and actresses. In a sense "actors and actresses" live in most of us. We see in supermarkets the many creams and other chemical products to help people look beautiful. Also, there are hundreds of magazines that advertise and promote beauty products which are often expensive. Not all, but usage of some of the so-called beauty products can even harm our skin. It is also not uncommon for people to undergo cosmetic surgeries.

However, most probably, Stephen did not spend any money buying any "beauty product" to make his face look like that of an angel. Further, he probably wouldn't have spent much time decorating himself in front of a mirror just before he was stoned. Still his face shined, his face was glorious, and it was beautiful – like that of an angel. So, what made Stephen's face look beautiful?

These are the secrets which really made Stephen look like an angel.

Listening to others makes us beautiful
In a self-centered world many like to be listened to. Stephen

was someone who listened to others. The Book of Acts (chapter 6) tells us that he was a compassionate and caring person. He listened to the needs of the impoverished. Furthermore, he not only listened to those who agreed with his faith in God in Christ but he also listened to those who disagreed with him.

God has given us two ears to listen and one mouth to speak. Perhaps this means that we need to listen twice as much as we speak but we often get this the wrong way around. Great leaders in the Bible were people who listened to God as well as to others. Abraham, Deborah, Martha's sister Mary and the disciples are to mention a few examples alongside Stephen. People of the early church too listened to each other and enjoyed the fellowship of one another. On the day of Pentecost people even understood others who spoke different languages. Perhaps they were so passionate to listen that the words, along with their body language, made sense.

Jesus Himself was a great listener. He listened to everyone who wanted to speak to Him. He listened to a blind man calling Him even in a busy and crowded street. In John 4 we read the conversation of Jesus and a Samaritan woman. Jesus listened and listened to all that she had to say. If you look at John 4 you will see that the first half of the chapter is mostly the woman speaking and Jesus listening. When we listen to others, they will know that we are interested in them and we have a concern for them. Listening is essential in building relationships. Listening can be a component that makes us look beautiful.

Speaking kind words makes us look beautiful

When we read about Stephen in the Bible another quality that stands out are his kind words. The Bible tells us that the words of Stephen were full of wisdom and full of the Spirit of God.[19] So, it's the words he spoke that made him look beautiful too. Stephen's words were words of kindness, goodness and they were about God.

You might know this familiar verse in the Book of Isaiah[20] and later repeated in the Book of Romans[21] – How beautiful are the feet of the ones who bring good news. Isaiah takes this analogy from war contexts. In those days, before people had phones or other instant communication technology, someone had to run on mountains, wilderness and dirty as well as thorny paths for days to bring the good news of victory to the people who were waiting. Literally speaking, the feet of the messenger who carried the good news of victory would be filthy and often bloody from walking on thorny paths. Nevertheless, Isaiah says "how beautiful are the feet of the one who brings good news." Why? It is the news they bring and the words they speak that make their feet look beautiful. Similarly, Stephen's words about God's victory in and through the death and resurrection of Jesus, made him look beautiful. Our words about God's goodness and mercy, too, can make us look beautiful.

We use many words every day. But we often don't realize that our words are important and powerful. At times, words can change lives. Words of comfort, encouragement and truth can make a big difference. Words of hope can empower and transform lives. Words of inspiration, words of love, words of faith and words of hope can bring joy and new life to people. For example, a doctor can hasten the recovery of a patient by assuring him/her that s/he is really improving.

Now, where did Stephen speak? He spoke at a synagogue as well as before the council. This shows us that we need to inquire after God in all aspects of our life – in our workplaces, in our families and in our communities. Biblically, our entire life should be an act of thanks offering to God. Stephen's words even in a tough situation of standing before the council were loud, clear and full of wisdom and they were about God.

Significantly, Paul – who wrote most of the letters in the New Testament – was present during the talk of Stephen. Paul saw Stephen being stoned and he also saw Stephen's face shining beautifully. It was immediately after Stephen's speech and the stoning of Stephen, that Paul left for Damascus. It is most likely that it was Stephen's words and shinning face that opened the eyes, ears and heart of Paul to Christ – through Jesus' light and voice on his way to Damascus. Stephen spoke with kindness, with divine energy and with scriptural authority. He spoke about God's guidance in the life of Abraham, Isaac, Jacob, Joseph, Moses and Joshua. His words made him look beautiful.

Words matter. Harsh words can be harmful, but kind words can be life affirming. Our choice of words reveals whether we are beautiful inside or not. We can follow the example of Stephen in our choice of words and decide to use kind words which go to make us beautiful.

St. Stephen's kind deeds made him look beautiful too

Even the early church formed by the apostles was not without problems. They had the practice of distributing food to the needy in the Church. The Church was growing remarkably but the distribution of food became unmanageable. But God's spirit guided them to solve the problem. They decided to share the responsibilities of the church. Stephen is introduced to us in this context. He was a person of good standing and he was on the rotas for helping the needy and sharing food to the poor. Thus, we know that it's not only the words but also the good deeds he did that brought beauty to his face.

So, we can ask ourselves what are the deeds we could do that would make us look beautiful. Good deeds will make you and me look beautiful.

Forgiveness makes us beautiful

Stephen, following the example of Jesus on the cross, forgives those who wanted him dead. Will I? Will you? Stephen even prays for them.

When we carry hurt and bitterness it affects us and not the offender. It might be genuine anger – it might be something unforgivable that someone has done against you but when we forgive we feel lighter and become beautiful inside. And sometimes it is not others we need to forgive, it is ourselves. Forgiving oneself is sometimes very hard too. However, when we ask God for help, we are given grace. It might take a lot of time but we shall get there eventually.

Joseph was betrayed and sold by his brothers. It must have been hard. It takes time to forgive. Forgiveness is often a process. However, he decided to forgive. He let his anger go, buried his hurt, gave it a funeral and did not dig it back up again. Here we see a model of how forgiveness works.

Forgiveness is not saying that all is well. We do acknowledge that wrong has been done but we ask God to do the needful. We decide to let go. A 14-year-old boy once told me that he had an alcoholic father, he grew up in an abusive home and he was uncared for and neglected Thankfully, he decided to forgive. He said, "the day I forgave I felt like I was released from a prison."

In no way do I want to downplay the difficulties that need to be surmounted for forgiveness We are called to pray to God to reform those who are disposed to commit felonies. In this context, it is worth recalling that the wife of Graham Staines, a Christian missionary forgave the killing of her husband and two children. Her forgiveness has reaffirmed that forgiveness is indeed a Christian virtue. As the Lord's Prayer implies, God forgives us when we forgive others and ourselves. And when God forgives, all is forgiven indeed.

Beauty is inside. Inside beauty will radiate on our faces. Forgiveness brought a shining face to Stephen. It will to you and me too.

I think all the things mentioned above: listening, speaking, kind words, deeds, and forgiving are all just practical demonstrations of the nine fruits of the spirit in Galatians 5. So, the key to being beautiful on the inside is being filled with the Spirit. And the key to showing it on the outside is a life of love, love for God and love for our neighbors.

So how do we know if we have succeeded? We will automatically have inner peace, trusting God and shine like a bright star. Our whole being will exude positive energy despite our difficulties in life.

We have explored the different features which can make us beautiful and build relationships in this sub-chapter. We will continue with the important theme of relating to one another in the next sub-chapter. We shall do that specifically considering the role of the church.

Questions for reflection or discussion

1. We look at the mirror to see if we are presentable to the outside world. How can we know if our hearts are beautiful?
2. How can we develop the art of listening?
3. Can you remember a time when someone's words hurt you? What advice would you give to that person?
4. How can we train ourselves to use words of kindness and encouragement?
5. Stephen's good deeds helped his church. What are the needs in your church and community?
6. Why do people find it hard to forgive?
7. Why do we need to forgive?

2.3 Together we are the Church

And he has put all things under his feet and has made him the head over all things for the church, which is his body, the fullness of him who fills all in all.[22]

The church must suffer for speaking the truth, for pointing out sin,

for uprooting sin. No one wants to have a sore spot touched, and therefore a society with so many sores twitches when someone has the courage to touch it and say: You have to treat that. You have to get rid of that. Believe in Christ. Be converted.
(Oscar A. Romero)

We are created to grow together under God. Being part of the church is not just our duty but also our joy.

Of course, the primary purpose of the church is to worship God and renew our relationship with God together. We have already seen the significance of worship life in the previous chapter. Thankfully, there are many faithful people all over the world who know what the church is for. There are people who rightly believe that the Church is a spiritual reality and that the Church is a new creation. They believe that when you come into a church fellowship, one of the things you should realize is you are entering a new world – a world of life and love – a new set of relationships, a new set of expectations of yourself and one another, and overpoweringly, a new sense of what God makes possible.

The faithful church goers of the past wanted people to have some sense of being out of their depth when they came into church – some sense of being surrounded and filled by glory, by something different, something that enabled them to look at everything they were taking for granted from a different angle. They wanted people in church to experience a foretaste of heaven at worshipping together.

We learn to read the word of God, the Bible, we learn to pray, we learn to sing praises to God, we learn to confess our sins and guilt, we learn to give thanks – acknowledging that we need God and one another, and we learn that we are created for eternity. At church we look at God's holiness and his light and the hope that God gives us.

A guidance document points out that the church, in concept

and practice, exists "to give glory to God through united and common witness and proclamation of the Gospel of our Lord Jesus Christ; to strengthen and further the Church's fellowship and make disciples of all nations. Further, the church exists to minister the doctrine and sacraments and discipline of Christ; and to uphold justice, responding vigorously to human needs by service; and striving to transform unjust structures of society, caring for God's creation and establishing the values of the Kingdom."[23]

When we become part of the church, we also become a witness to each other. When others see us, they know that they are not alone in their faith journey. We human beings naturally seek love and encouragement from others. Living Christianly includes a life of witness and mutual encouragement to grow in our faith in God. As you know, fire in a log is put out easily but logs burn better together. Church is where we learn to shine together for God in Christ.

The only way to know, experience, dwell and receive the power of God which flows into His church is by being part of it. At church we learn together that we all are children of the same heavenly father. Often the church is called a family – indeed, the church is a family of God literally. In fact, we all are children of the same heavenly father.

Church is for everyone

At church, when people praise God together, we feel a sense of oneness. When we pray together, read the biblical verses together and sing hymns together, we not only derive a new strength in Christ, but also realize our need for being with one another to be the church. Thus, Jesus prays, "that *all of them may be one*, Father, just as you are in me and I am in you ... I have given the glory that you gave me, that *they may be one* as we are one."[24] This teaches us that the church is for everyone.

Bonhoeffer pointed out, "It is the unity of the whole church which makes each member what he is and the fellowship what it is, just as it is Christ and his Body which makes the Church what it is."[25]

Unlike many clubs which are for members alone, the Church is for everyone. All are welcome at church. Many people of the church in the past considered that being part of a church family was an integral part of life and rightly and beneficially so.

Growing together

The church is expected to be a model of peace, trust and justice where everyone exemplifies how to live a life in dialogue, engagement and love. The church believes all that we have is a gift. And we learn to share those gifts responsibly and generously seeking the good of each other. In other words, the church has to be a foretaste of heaven.

The church, by definition, is unconditionally inclusive because God is inclusive – inclusive in its welcome but also its commitment. The church must be generous in its love for one another because God is generous in His love for us. Even though God hates sin, He loves sinners.

The church responds positively to common good. This not only helps communities but also brings people of the church family closer as they spend time with each other and work together.

Sacraments: Baptism

In the New Testament, baptism is seen as a decision-making time. Baptism is an event at which the believer decides to become a follower of Jesus. The Church today rightly welcomes people into the Church (i.e., the body of Christ) through baptism.

Paul tells us that we all are baptized into one body.

For just as the body is one and has many members, and all the members of the body, though many, are one body, so it is with Christ. For in the one Spirit we were all baptized into one body—Jews or Greeks, slaves or free—and we were all made to drink of one Spirit

... If one member suffers, all suffer together with it; if one member is honoured, all rejoice together with it, all rejoice together. Now you are the body of Christ and individually members of it.[26]

Baptism is a moment of grace at which we receive new life from Christ. It also marks the beginning of becoming part of the Church. If you are already baptized – Congratulations! If not, what is stopping you?

Holy Communion

Holy Communion is the meal initiated by Jesus Himself. Just as we need food to nourish us physically, Holy Communion nourishes us spiritually. Our taste buds tell us what our food tastes like. Our spiritual taste buds are what taste the love of God in Christ and we have a glimpse of new life in Christ when we taste the meal of Holy Communion.

When we come together to receive our spiritual sustenance from the same cup it is once again a powerful symbol of unity, equality and mutuality. So, Holy Communion not only renews our relationship with God but when we receive from the same cup we renew and strengthen our relationship with each other too.

Being part of the Church is being part of its mission and ministry

The Church today carries out its ministry in a rapidly changing political, social and cultural world. This pressure constantly calls the Church to continue its mission. When we pray and reflect on the mission of the Church together, we will find God's plan for His church being fulfilled in and through you and me.

Ministry involves a dynamic tension between receptivity and activity. All of us are recipients of God's grace, through word and sacrament. But all of us are also called to act: sent forth to proclaim liberty to the captives and recovery of sight to the blind, to set free the oppressed and announce that the time has come when the Lord will save his people to live lives that are signs of God's coming reign. Being part of the church is to live out this life following the example of Jesus.

The ministry of the church involves the whole people of God, and it is not to be left to those who have been ordained to the office of the ministry or called to special tasks within the church. It is the participation of all people in the ministry that goes to make the mission of the church more effective and more fruitful. The constant interaction between the laity and the clergy is what lends strength to the church. The role of the "ordinary members of the church" is no less important than those who are tasked with priestly responsibilities. The church can and should send out the message of unity to the wider world.

Church – A model of unity

To be a church is to break through the sociological barriers of status. Christ wants us to break through these barriers. Christian fellowship breaches all boundaries of class and makes us "Christians-in-arms." Jesus wants to turn our world upside down. If he were telling the story today – he would have said – invite the outcasts, the people affected with AIDS, the street children, the orphans, the bonded laborers, the destitute and the victims of war.

Even today, we live in a world where many may not want to invite Jesus for dinner because he may cause embarrassment and unease. But then it falls on them to see that He does not make them feel uneasy, uncomfortable and embarrassed. They should give up their old ways and learn to look at life and people around them as Christ does.

Jesus invites everyone for His Grand Banquet. He invites all of us, from all cultures, backgrounds, classes and castes to the great feast, the Lord's Supper, the unique feast none of us can repay. God's light was fully shone in Jesus that he saw his brothers and sisters among all people including the poor, the needy and the ostracized.

Working together

There are at least five things to take on board. First of all, when we are involved in God's ministry, we need to know that we are serving God and His people and not ourselves. We need to know that we are not alone. We are parts of Christ's body and He is the head. If we don't remember – that we work for God and His people and not for ourselves – we could be put off by others' criticisms, or when the workload becomes heavier, we could lose interest.

Second, we also need to keep in our mind that our goal is the same. Hence, we need to focus on what we have in common and our similarities not on our differences. Paul says, "Let us concentrate on the things which make for harmony, and on the growth of one another's character."[27] As people of God we share one Lord, one body, one purpose, one Father, one Spirit, one hope, one faith, one baptism and one love. We share the same salvation, the same life, and the same future – factors far more important than any differences we could enumerate.

Third, as we work together let us also be realistic in our expectations of each other. Otherwise, we will become dispirited. God is perfect but the church is not. The reason is because we are not perfect. The central thought should be that we are striving to grow together to become like Christ. And we do need to give thanks for the Christian fellowship in which we are blessed to have been placed. We should be humble enough to admit that we have no great wisdom but a lot of weakness. Still by God's grace we can acquire enough wisdom and strength to grow in fellowship. All members of the church must make it a habit to encourage others and refrain from criticizing others. But then "positive criticism" made in the right spirit can be valuable too.

Fourth, Jesus sees church as a place which can model unity and togetherness and hence, he says if there is a conflict take it to the church and sort it out. So, we are to play the role of mediators between people who are in conflict and comforters to those who are hurt. While there is nothing wrong in having the "attainment of happiness" as a goal what is far more important is that we should be able to lead a truly Christian life.

Finally, Paul invites the Colossians to work in harmony and work together for a specific purpose. He calls them to work together to experience God in newer ways.

Church is the Body of Christ and the Bride of Christ

Above all, the church is one body. It is the body of Christ. Each part of our body is connected with one another. Each supports the other and all parts work together. They are related to each other. Jesus is the head of the Church. We are all parts of the same body, says Paul. For Paul, being a member of the church meant being a vital organ of a living body. This means the church is an organism pulsating with life.

This is important because only as participating members can we learn to care about each other and share the experiences of others. If one part of the body suffers, all the other parts suffer with it too. Or if one part of our body is honored all the other parts share its honor.

There is no other human relationship that brings us together as a community because we relate with one another in church at a deeper level. Our bond is glued and bolstered by our common faith in God. We are glued together and made cheerful by the hope we always have in God.

In our world which is divided and fractured, one clear role which the church plays or is called to play, is to hold all humanity together. This is because God lives in all. When we see others, we need to see God in them. Sometimes it is easy and other times it is difficult but the church is there, amongst other things, to help us to live in a community under God.

Also, just as the two partners in a married relationship are committed to each other, God in Jesus is committed to His church. He expects the church to be committed to Him. No wonder the church is called the bride of Christ. We together make the bride of Christ, anticipating (and looking forward to) the joy of a life with God.

Having looked at the role of the church in building relationships in this sub-chapter, we will move on to explore how we can engage with people of different religions in the next section.

Questions for reflection or discussion

1. What do you think are the purposes of the church?
2. Is the church different from other clubs in society? If yes, how?
3. Christians know that the church is for everyone. However, why do some people choose not to be part of the church?
4. How do sacraments help a believer grow closer to God and to other believers?
5. How can the church promote unity in local communities?
6. If we understand the church as the body of Christ literally, what would the church look like?
7. What does it mean to say that the church is the bride of Christ?

2.4 Engaging with people of different faiths and no faith

You will seek me and find me when you seek me with all your heart.[28]

God's love supersedes all religions and it is the core of all religions.
(Riaz Ahmed Gohar Shahi)

We looked at the role of the church in connecting with one another in the last sub-chapter. Here, we will look at ways in which we can relate to people of other religions. God in Jesus engaged with people of different faiths with love and compassion. For example, Jesus crossed the boundaries of religion and culture and helped a Roman centurion. He healed a Syrophoenician girl. He voluntarily went to a Samaritan village which no Jew, during His time, did. He entered into conversation with a Samaritan woman with confidence, compassion and love.

We live in the same world where people of different faiths and no faith co-exist. God in Jesus did not just stick with people adhering to His religious culture alone. He loved everyone despite what they believed or believed in. Jesus here sets a model of ministry for us. Because God loves all people regardless of their beliefs and practices, we all need to do the same.

Exclusivism, Inclusivism, Pluralism and Dialogue
There are four stances which people generally take when it comes to engaging with people of different religions and no religion.

First is the exclusivist position. Exclusivists believe that their religion is the right one and the religions of others are all wrong. Exclusivists only have something to tell others, nothing to learn from others, and they don't see reality as broader than themselves and their own religion.

Second is the inclusivist stance. Inclusivists, too, believe that their religion is the right one. However, they have a strong desire to include people of other religions and no religion into their faith community.

Third, we look at pluralism. Pluralists construe that truth doesn't really belong to one religion or another. It gives freedom to everyone to have their own beliefs and practices. This creates a situation in which it does not become possible to learn and change our lives by interacting with them since the need for it does not arise in a pluralist culture.

Fourth, we see people who promote dialogue and conversation.

Jesus certainly did engage with people of different religions through listening and talking. We will look at how he engaged with a Samaritan woman in this session.

Further, we see Paul engaging in conversation with Jews and his Greco-Roman counterparts giving us a model for interfaith dialogue.[29] It is worth noting that today in both Roman Catholic circles and in Protestant circles the need for inter-religious conversation is stressed. This was well emphasized in the Vatican II, a Roman Catholic conference.[30] The conference emphasized, "Dialogue is a two-way communication. It implies speaking and listening, giving and receiving, for mutual growth and enrichment. It includes witness to one's own faith as well as an openness to that of the other. It is not a betrayal of mission of the Church, nor is it a new method of conversion to Christianity. This has been clearly stated in the encyclical letter of Pope John Paul II *Redemptoris Missio*. This view is also developed in the two documents produced by the PCID (Pontifical Council for Interreligious Dialogue): The Attitude of the Catholic Church towards the Followers of Other Religious Traditions: reflections on Dialogue and Mission (1984), Dialogue and Proclamation (1991)."[31] Similarly a publication of the World Council of Churches says, "We feel able with integrity to assure our partners in dialogue that we come not as manipulators but as fellow pilgrims."[32] It is true that in the conversation of beliefs and practices between people of different faiths and no faith one becomes more aware of oneself as well as what really happens in God's world.

Listening as engaging

In John 4, we see Jesus breaching a socio-religious boundary. Although he was a Jew, He entered into conversation with a Samaritan woman, which was very uncommon during His time.

Precisely, we see the time which Jesus gives to listen in John 4. He could have started by saying – I am the Messiah – if you give me water I will give you living water, and finished there. But he wanted to listen to the Samaritan woman. He just says, "Give me a drink" and waits for her response. The conversation begins in verse 7. But, only in verse 10 does He talk about living water, which is fullness of life and only in verse 26 He says, "I am the Messiah."

Often, we just want to tell others what we think and we give less time listening to them. Here, we learn from Jesus that taking time to listen is as important as sharing our faith stories with others.

In the context of inter-religious dialogue, some just try to impose their ideas on others and give little importance and time to listening. They just say – your belief is untrue and wrong – and mine is true and right. It might or might not be the truth. But, Jesus before talking about living water or anything else, builds a relationship through conversation. Again, He just added the word – living – to water, which the woman could readily relate to. There is give and take.

It is about building relationships. And to build relationships we need to listen. Of course, listening to others takes time. Building relationships is essential in our social life. One man complained about his children. He said, "I provide everything they need. What more could they want?" He wife replied, "They want us, our ears, our attention, our presence and our time." In fact, whenever we give our time, we are expressing our devotion to them and devotion is the essence of love. Taking time to listen to others is a precious gift we can give them.

The Samaritan woman, too, very attentively listened to Jesus. She was convinced that His words were useful and were of eternal significance.

Engaging through Dialogue

Obviously, God has blessed us with a world where people of different religious persuasions and no religious inclination co-exist. We need to engage in dialogue because it is in conversation that we understand people of different faiths and no faith better. It is a pre-requisite that we need to be aware of the viewpoints of others if we want to engage with them.

Firstly, inter-faith dialogue not only points out similarities between the two cultures represented by two persons engaged in conversation, but also portrays differences. In other words, similarities and differences become explicit and come to the fore in inter-faith conversation.

Secondly, inter-faith dialogue helps in forming a greater understanding about truth. A worldview constructed without dialogue can portray only one side of truth. It is in conversation that the manifold challenges of truth are revealed. These revealed challenges will lead us to grasp what truth is and embrace it with prayer and knowledge. In the process of conversation, we often change too.

Thirdly, inter-faith conversation is a dynamic on-going process not only because beliefs keep changing but also because people change.

Fourthly, our dialogue needs to be positive. Positive conversation is based on a healthy respect for different faiths and no faith involved in the process. Sometimes conflicts and acts of violence occur due to no dialogue or shallow dialogues. Religious fundamentalism does not allow proper dialogue to take place. The need for a tolerant, open-minded or positive conversation becomes apparent here. The need to engage with others in a true and deeper manner cannot be over-emphasized.

Fifthly, it is through dialogue that mutual enrichment becomes possible. God-talk in our world can be assorted with diverse perspectives since people of different faiths and beliefs make the world context. It might not be wrong to be inclined to think that God speaks through the diverse cultures of our world to mutually enrich each other.

The big question now is whether a Christian can be faithful

to Christ as well as open to other religious traditions. I believe that it is possible. We have seen the limitations of exclusivism, inclusivism and pluralism. Engaging with others through conversation is an expression of our love for others. God in Christ transcended boundaries of faith because He loved people unconditionally. We need to do the same.

The issue of Religious Conversion

Apparently, the problem of conversion has been dogging people for centuries now. Though dialogue is primarily a religious issue, it also has to do with the social, economic, political and psychological challenges of life.

God in Jesus respected people of different religious traditions for who they were. Regarding the process of inter-religious conversation, we too should respect the integrity of different traditions. Being open to learn from others and be subject to change in the process of understanding truth better, is immensely significant.

In this light, conversion, first, should be decided by our knowledge and thought and not based on our traditional embeddedness, but on the basis of God's revelation to us.

Second, conversion should not be the goal of people who engage in conversation, rather the goal is inter-religious harmony. Conversion should be decided by each individual, family or community, based on inter-religious conversation.

Third, conversion is a voluntary decision to be made over against proselytization. This too is applicable to individuals, families or communities.

Fourth, any inducements made for conversion cannot be countenanced in a world where free choice is a basic human right. We need to squarely prohibit induced conversion.

And fifth, conversions motivated by any kind of non-voluntary action are not commensurate with the values of Scripture. They are alien to the Christian tenets enunciated in the Scripture.

Inter-faith ministry is not an option

In our multi-religious world, God doesn't want us to ignore people of different faiths and no faith. As we saw earlier, we are all inter-connected and form an organic whole. God wants us to share His love and light beyond all boundaries. Inter-faith ministry is not an optional extra but at the very core of a life of togetherness in this world.

We have discussed the pertinent issue of inter-faith relationships in this section. In the next section, we will learn about our place in the wider world and how we could relate with the wider creation.

Questions for discussion or reflection

1. What can we learn from Jesus in relation to interfaith ministry?
2. Can one learn one's own faith tradition better by engaging with another religious tradition?
3. Why is listening very important in interfaith dialogue?
4. Do you think churches take interfaith ministry seriously? Why should churches engage in the interfaith mission?
5. Do you think you are an exclusivist or inclusivist or pluralist or someone who is open to dialogue? And why?
6. Why should we aim for mutual enrichment when we dialogue with people of different faiths?

2.5 Stewards of God's Creation

Praise the Lord from the earth, you great sea creatures and all ocean depths, lightning and hail, snow and clouds, stormy winds that do his bidding, you mountains and all hills, fruit trees and all cedars, wild animals and all cattle, small creatures and flying birds, kings of the earth and all nations, you princes and all rulers on earth, young men and maidens, old men and children. Let them praise the name of the Lord, for his name alone is exalted.[33]

We all draw breath and life from the same source of creation.
(Bryant McGill, *Voice of Reason*)

God created the universe out of nothing. God delights when we take care of the creation that has been entrusted into our hands. God wants us to respect and care for the universe. We are stewards of God's creation.

Significantly, even during the destruction in Noah's time, it was not only humanity which was saved by God's orders. Noah was told by God to protect every species. This Old Testament episode tells us that God loves His entire creation and not just humanity.

Further, the Bible says that not even one sparrow will fall to the ground apart from the will of God.[34] God's concern for nature creates an obligation in us to care for His creation. In fact, the inter-dependency between humanity and nature is what sustains them both.

Again, with regard to Jesus' teachings, it should be pointed out that in almost all parables, the kingdom of God message is taught with the help of imageries drawn from the wider creation. To mention a few: the parable of the shepherd and the sheep (John 10: 1–39), the parable of mustard seed (Matthew 13: 13-38) and the parable of the sower (Matthew 13: 18–30). We should bear in mind that at the time of Jesus, ecological destruction was not a big challenge as it is today. His teaching would probably put greater focus on our stewardship of the creation if His time were faced with an environmental crisis as the contemporary world is faced with.

Paul believes that precisely in Christ the entire universe is held together. In his words, "He [Christ] is before all things, and in Him all things hold together."[35]

Seeing glimpses of God in His Creation
Biblically and traditionally, it is often understood that God

created humanity in His image which is true. Of course, God says through the Bible that you and I are created in His image but this does not mean that the wider creation doesn't have any glimpse of God's image in them. In fact, we need to see glimpses of God's image (at least in a lesser level) in the wider creation too.

The truth is that today we know that a language trained bonobo exhibits flashes of intelligence akin to those of a human child. I think we are prejudiced when we say that only we have the image of God in us. We are only a little more intelligent than other beings. We cannot claim monopoly over intelligence and rule out the possibility of other beings having intelligence. The level of intelligence varies from person to person; to put it in a lighter vein, it can vary from species to species too.

Paul speaks of the redemption of all creation.[36] In this context, salvation only to human beings is no longer relevant. It needs to be corrected by seeing the need for the salvation of nature as a whole. There is no corner of the earth that does not need the salvation assured on the cross. We, as responsible beings, must acknowledge our previous narrow understanding that we alone are created for eternity.

We need to open our eyes for glimpses of God in things He created. We cannot limit God's image or love only to us anymore. The privilege of having God's love is not limited to humanity; it extends to all creations.

Our spirituality should include a concern for a strong and well-balanced human-nature relationship. The rationale is that God seeks to be in a harmonious relationship with the entire creation. Ecological systems are not to be damaged or destroyed but are to be taken care of and nurtured.

Caring for God's Creation

So, what are our responsibilities and how can we today perform them? Scripture has a number of significant references to the environment. Such references might help us discern the problems we face today and find suitable solutions for them. Across much of the Old Testament humanity is given considerable authority over the natural world. For example, it says, "Yet you made them only a little lower than God and crowned them with glory and honour. You gave them charge of everything you made, putting all things under their authority — the flocks and the herds and all the wild animals, the birds in the sky, the fish in the sea, and everything that swims the ocean currents."[37] The Old Testament is an affirmation that creation was an act of God and as such all of creation is His.[38] He reminds Job of this as follows: "Where were you when I laid the foundation of the earth? Tell me, if you have understanding."[39] Psalm 50:10–12 attests to this proposition, "For every wild animal of the forest is mine, the cattle on a thousand hills. I know all the birds of the air, and all that moves in the field is mine. If I were hungry, I would not tell you, for the world and all that is in it is mine."[40]

Moreover, the psalmist lays great emphasis on the greatness of God in relation to all that He has created.[41] Similarly Psalm 36:9 acknowledges that life springs from God and describes Him as the living spring. Psalm 65:9–13 is an expression of gratefulness to God for his provision of the appropriate seasons and climate in order that there is sufficient food and produce to be shared with the recognition that all the provision is from God alone.

As we noted earlier, we know that God was concerned for His creation as He instructed Noah to take two of every living creature aboard the ark, but He also gave Noah and His family charge over all of them, expecting them to care for every living creature. Noah was a staunch believer and a righteous man and his life was spared for this reason.

If humanity was to put God at the center of everything rather than putting itself at the center, it might help towards having greater respect for nature. By bringing God into the center we are also respecting Him and remembering Him as creator of all, including the future. Therefore, in order to protect the future for generations to come we need to protect the present and where possible steward the creation.

As continents, nations, communities, groups and individuals, we need to heed God's warnings. If we keep God before us, we need to preserve the world we are entrusted with.[42] We need to preserve the rivers, before they become deserts.[43] If we turn back to God in right relationship with him there is hope.[44] This prophesy that was pertinent to the Israelites is pertinent to us too. At the present juncture when the need for preserving the environment is greater than ever before we are called to lend our voices and take concerted actions to advance the cause of the preservation of the environment. What we do may appear to be small, but it does indeed go towards making a big difference.

In the Genesis story we read that everything that God created was good. Therefore, it becomes incumbent upon us to limit, take control of and avoid all actions that exploit, pollute and degrade the earth. The biblical creation story is one that is of transition from chaos to order. For that reason, we should not allow the environment to slide into chaos. We should preserve the "order" as put in place by God. Toward this end there should be collaborative efforts by scientists, social activists, social planners and political leaders.

The recent Covid-19 pandemic, although it was horrible and deadly in many ways, has also taught us that we can make a positive difference to the environment God has placed us in. You and I need to join hands with those working towards a more ecological or "green" lifestyle. The causes for the ecological crisis have to be tackled collectively by the global community. Organizations such as A Rocha, The Jubilee Center, The Faraday Institute for Science and Religion, The John Ray Initiative (JRI), Tearfund and World Vision to name but a few are actively engaged in efforts to save the planet, of which we too have an obligation to be part of. There is no option to choosing greener energy. Being energy savvy by taking simple measures such as unplugging items that are not in use, hanging out washing not tumble drying, wearing extra jumpers rather than turning the heating up are some of the many ways of being energy efficient. Energy can be used efficiently and, in the process, saved by adopting simple measures such as walking, using local shops, car sharing/using electric vehicles/public transport, growing produce for self-sufficiency and being part of a produce co-operative.

Similarly, we can purchase food produced without chemical use locally and ethically. We could choose food produced organically or with minimal chemical use. This is good not only for the environment but also for our health.

Harming animals is prohibited and rightly so. No one should harm them. By becoming vegetarian or restricting meat consumption we can serve the cause of the environment. In our homes we should avoid excessive waste by purchasing carefully and being thrifty with spare food. We should ensure to minimise the use of chemicals in the home or garden by using natural alternatives. Needless to say, we should certainly recycle and reuse.

Communities and society at-large can endeavor to follow the A Rocha Eco – Church award scheme, use Green Energy suppliers, create eco-friendly gardens, and use eco products.

God dwells within us and amongst us; stewardship of the earth in action and love is integral to sustaining creation and part of God's law. We need to live as if each day were our last. We need to look after the earth as we are part of it and not apart from nature. We need to look after the earth as it is not only the home of the present generation but for posterity too.

In this chapter, we have explored that we are created to relate with others and other beings too. We were also created by God to live out our full potential in terms of our career, discipleship and mission. This is another important dimension in our life. We move on to learn about this in the next chapter.

Questions for reflection or discussion

1. God loves His creation. In what ways can we join God in loving His creation?
2. How can we develop our eyes to see God's glory in His creation around us?
3. Do you think salvation is just for humanity or for all creation?
4. We are dependent on all creatures and nature around us. Can you think of a few examples to prove this point?
5. What are some of the ways we can be good stewards of God's creation?
6. Planting trees and feeding birds are two examples of caring for creation. Can you think of a few other ways we can help sustain our environment?

Chapter 3

Life Is the Only Opportunity—God-Inspired Life Is to Be and Become Who You Really Are

3.1 Prayer and discernment

Show me your ways, Lord, teach me your paths. Guide me in your truth and teach me, for you are God my Savior and my hope is in you all day long.[1]

Take, Lord, and receive all my liberty, my memory, my understanding, and my entire will, all I have and call my own. You have given all to me. To you, Lord, I return it. Everything is yours; do with it what you will. Give me only your love and your grace, that is enough for me.
(St. Ignatius of Loyola)

In the last chapter, we looked at God's desire for us in terms of relating with one another. The truth is God has created us with so much potential for good within us. God rejoices when you and I are instruments, not in our own hands, but in His hands. We will explore this crucial dimension in this chapter.

Being an instrument in God's hands is initiated when we commit ourselves into God's hands in prayer every day. We can begin each day by praying, "Help me to be with you Lord today and walk in your ways. In Jesus' name. Amen." God takes over when we give ourselves, in prayer, into His hands. Indeed, God not only created you and me, but He also loves to lead us through our everyday lives.

Each one of us is made with different skills and strengths. Each one of us is given different talents. Each one of us is unique, special and of infinite worth in the eyes of God. The best thing to do is to ask God to help you to be the person He really made you to be and to do your best that day.

Obviously, God's will for us is that we will put our trust in Him and come closer to Him day by day. The prophet Micah puts it succinctly, "He has told you, O mortal, what is good; and what does the LORD require of you but to do justice, and to love kindness, and to walk humbly with your God?"[2]

God's will is that we will live in obedience to His word. Jesus not only came to give himself for us but also to show us how to live a life filled with love, righteousness, justice, integrity, kindness and compassion.

Life is short and it is our one and only God-given opportunity. Prayer is at the heart of discerning how to make the best use of this opportunity. When we pray God listens to us. His plans are better for us than our own plans for ourselves. What we need to do is to trust God.

Prayer is at the heart of discernment

Prayer is simply listening to God and talking with Him. If a marriage is to work well there needs to be good communication. If a company or an organization is to work well good communication is key. If communication fails in a company everybody will start doing what they want to rather than what is best for the company to be productive and fruitful. Similarly, it is through listening to God and talking with Him that we become the God-loving people He wants us to be.

The Book of Daniel and particularly the incident of Daniel in the lions' den might sound familiar to you. Or you might say, oh, Daniel in the lions' den – that's a continuing favorite children's story. Of course, there are books with beautiful pictures with Daniel surrounded by lions and lionesses which will stay in children's minds for a long time. Yet, there is so much more to Daniel than a familiar or a favorite story. Daniel, a man of prayer teaches both children and adults alike lessons about life and how to live a God-inspired life – discerned through prayer.

Daniel prayed three times a day. Prayer did not keep him away from the lions' den, but God was with him even in the most dangerous lions' den. Do you take prayer seriously? How often do you pray? Do you have a regular time for prayer? Prayer is the first thing we need to do as we begin our day. And pray that God will lead you in His ways, fulfilling His purposes in and through you that day to be the best you can be. Prayer has the power to change your day for the better. Prayer has the power to help you live Christianly, constructively, creatively and fruitfully. You can pause throughout the day to pray for God's guidance and strength. You can end your day by thanking God for fulfilling His purposes for you that day.

The life of Daniel teaches us that prayer is the backbone of a God-inspired life. There is no substitute for prayer. Further, it is not just the Book of Daniel but other books in the Old Testament (and the New Testament) that talk about the importance of prayer in relation to discernment. The gospel writers tell us that Jesus taught his disciples how to pray, the prayer we know as the Lord's Prayer. He taught His disciples to pray that God's will be done.

I can't emphasize enough the importance Jesus gives to prayer. On several occasions, Jesus taught his disciples the importance of prayer. For example, in one parable, Jesus says that if a friend keeps knocking at his friend's door – even if the friend has gone to bed – he will get up and give his friend what he needs. When we ask God for help in prayer, He helps us. God keeps His promises.

Jesus himself took time to pray to God the Father. Spending time with God in prayer will empower us and guide us. Perhaps we need to talk less and listen more to God. Spending time with God will also increase our peace and contentment so that people looking at us may see something of God's light in us.

Some of you might have a specific way of praying and filling yourself with God. And sometimes it takes a lot of time. A Bishop was found praying for about an hour. Someone was keeping an eye on him. At the end he was told, "You pray for a long time." The Bishop replied, "Oh no, I have prayed for about five minutes. But it took a long time to get through." He knew that no time we spend to connect with God in prayer will go to waste.

An agnostic asked Archbishop Temple if prayer made a difference or if it's all mere coincidences? He famously replied, "The more I pray the more the coincidences."[3] The more we pray the more the power we have. The power of godly discernment is a gift for those who pray.

I have read a book about the Sherpas, i.e., a group of people who took expeditions in the Himalayas. In one of the Himalayan expeditions, after several days of non-stop walking, and knowing the task that still lay ahead of them, the Sherpas simply sat down and would not go on. For a whole day, they sat and eventually they gave the reason that they had been going too fast and they had been trying to do too much and the thought of the task ahead of them troubled them more and more. They said their souls had not been able to keep up with them and now they were waiting for their souls to catch up with them.

Spending time doing nothing might not feel sufficiently active but Daniel and other people of God teach us the need for this, the need for our souls to catch up with us. Jesus too gives us an example of prayerful life – not the hyperactive prayer when we talk and talk and talk, but those times when we sit quietly and bring certain things into the presence of God without talking too much. So, the resolution for today could be – to pray more, to pray for ourselves, for others and for those who pray for us. As we reflect on life as the one and only opportunity, we can pray that God will help us not to miss this opportunity. Listening to God, in prayer is the best way to discern. Prayer helps us build a relationship with God. Discernment is impossible without listening to God. Taking time to pray and listening carefully to the voice of God through your inner ears is developed through practice and patience.

Points to remember when you pray

P – Pray that God will fill you with *Peace*. Without God's peace within us it is difficult to live out a God-inspired life.

R – Pray that God will grant you *Resilience*. Life has ups and downs. Resilience is a virtue, and we need to pray that God will give us the resilience we need to bounce back.

A – Pray that God will bless you with *Abilities*. When God blesses our abilities, we can go the second mile in His strength.

Y – Pray that you will say *Yes to God's Call*. It all begins when we say yes to God. Our prayer needs to be that we will answer positively to God's call in our life.

When we pray God helps us to be focused

Very often we think we do things with our strength but, in fact, the things we take for granted are given by grace. A woodpecker pecked and pecked. At the same time there was a great storm. The storm brought the tree down. Nonetheless, the woodpecker thought that its beak was strong. Just as the woodpecker thought we might also think that we have power in us but all that we do is through God-given power, mercy, strength and grace.

Life can be compared to a football match. When the match nears the end, the players get together and say, "There is only 10 minutes left, let us give our best." In other words, "Now is the time to play well so that we don't regret it later." It is similar in life. We have only one life. And our time is limited. We can ask God to help us focus on Him and His ways for us.

To sum up, on our death beds, when we look back at our life, would the things that we do or don't do today make us happy or miserable? Discernment is the art and science of knowing what

God does and joining Him.

Scripture and Tradition

Therefore, I urge you, brothers and sisters, in view of God's mercy, to offer your bodies as a living sacrifice, holy and pleasing to God — this is your true and proper worship. Do not conform to the pattern of this world, but be transformed by the renewing of your mind. Then you will be able to test and approve what God's will is — his good, pleasing and perfect will.[4]

As we saw earlier there is no substitute for prayer. There is no alternative for learning the word of God either. The Scripture teaches us the ways God wants us to walk. Meditating on God's word and being rooted in it will remind us of the ways God has guided and led His people in the past. God has not changed. God, through His word, guides us even today.

The Bible, in fact, is full of people of godly discernment. Judges discern, prophets discern, followers of Jesus discern and all spiritual giants discern. For example, Abraham was a man of abundant faith and great discernment. So, what did he do differently? He did not tell God – this is my plan for me and my family. Instead, he asked God what His plan was for him and his family. God told him to leave his country and go to the place He showed him. Abraham left his familiar culture, country, friends, and native town and went. That is discernment and obedience at their best.

Discernment can be easy at one time and hard at another time. Through the Scripture we learn that discernment can be a process. When we take time to learn the word of God, He begins to talk to us. We will discern His ways for us. The psalmist writes, "Your word is a lamp to my feet and a light to my path."[5]

No doubt, we could also learn from the life of God's people in the church's history. The testimonies of others, in the Bible, the early church and the present-day church help us to learn to trust that God's way for us is better than our way for ourselves. Discernment ultimately is about intimacy with God and living out the life that flows from God.

Where there is a need take it as a call from God

In the next sub-chapter, we will look at God's call in terms of our career. In the following sub-chapters, we will learn about God's will for us in terms of our discipleship, witness, mission and service. However, here we end by illustrating that when we see a need we need to take it as a call from above.

Robert Raikes who started Sunday school saw a few children getting bored and wasting their time. He organized the first Sunday school which included all subjects including the study of the Bible. A small beginning grew. Robert started with a handful of children. Today Sunday school is a worldwide movement – millions have found God in their lives through Sunday school. Robert's motto was when you see a need take it as a call from God. The beginning of Scouting and Guiding is similar. It was a response to addressing a need in the community.

Questions for reflection or discussion

1. How do you differentiate between what is from God and what is not?
2. What does prayer mean to you?
3. How can you grow in discernment?
4. Do you have a favorite character in the Bible who was great at discernment? If yes, what do you like about him or her?
5. Do you find discernment easy or hard?
6. Can you remember an occasion when the voice of God was clear to you?
7. What is the need in your own church? Do you see a need in the community? Do you sense any call in your life at the moment?

3.2 Created to be and to become.
But how do I choose?

Unless the LORD builds the house, those who build it labour in vain. Unless the LORD guards the city, the guard keeps watch in vain. It is in vain that you rise up early and go late to rest, eating the bread of anxious toil for he gives sleep to his beloved.[6]

Having looked at the significance of prayer, scripture and tradition in relation to discernment, we now proceed to reflect on our career life. At some point everyone faces the question of what they do with their life. What am I created for? Most people deal with this question of purpose in relation to work more than once as they journey through life. It is important to ask this question now and then to make sure we are on the right track in the eyes of God.

Nevertheless, talking about our work is different from the common call we all have for discipleship, witness and mission in our life. Indeed, our considerate living is more important to God than our career. We will devote the remaining three sessions in this chapter to look at the bigger and greater call of God in our life.

However, God is interested in our work life too. He wants us to do our best in our chosen field, with His help. Here we look at this dimension of life.

There are many routes to building our work life. Recently, I was at a local careers event in a big hall. I was amazed to see the advertisements pointing out the diverse and numerous career options out there in the world. Some people, who are ambitious and brave enough, will consider self-employment and start up a company or business of their own. And every day new ideas and innovations come into existence. It is logical and reasonable that we should work and earn our living if we are able to do so. If possible, we can create job opportunities so that others too will do their work and unlock their potential. God wants us to do our best to serve others in our life.

The Bible says, "For even when we were with you, we would give you this command: If anyone is not willing to work, let him not eat."[7]

I hasten to add what Paul means by this. Paul is writing this not to those who sadly are not able to work and earn their living but to those who can. Those who can't work due to ill health or because they are caring full-time for a person in need or any other genuine reasons need to be helped. It is God's will that those who are not able to work for whatever reason need to be supported fully. There are many biblical verses that teach us to share our resources with the needy and the poor.

However, most people, as we know, can work and earn their wages – pay their bills – and possibly save a little for rainy days.

So, first and foremost, we understand that work is not an option in life. When we work hard, we enjoy the benefits. In short, we need to trust God and work hard. God-led life is one which contributes to the local community and the wider society in all the creative, productive, enriching and rebuilding ways possible.

The big question now is, "How do I know what God wants me to do?" In a world of many good choices, how do I choose?

All life-edifying work is pleasing in the eyes of God. To give you a simple analogy, it doesn't matter whether we have beans or broccoli with our dinner. Both are healthy. God doesn't mind which vegetable we eat that day, but He does want us to eat healthy food. Similarly, God doesn't mind what work we do for a living as long as it is not demeaning others or harmful to anyone's health and growth. All constructive, creative and life-affirming work that promotes the common good is pleasing in the eyes of God. God is creative and He is the greatest healer, comforter and edifier. God is pleased when we work in constructive, creative and edifying ways. So, all work that affirms people's lives, brings glory to God and nurtures the welfare of His creation is acceptable in God's sight.

Jesus says that we are the salt of the earth and we are the light of the world.[8] Imagine you are in God's presence and He says these words to you directly: "You are the salt of the earth. You are the light of the world." How would the career you choose help you to be salt and light in this world? To live purposefully is to be "salt" and "light" in our world.

Enjoy what you do

For we are God's handiwork, created in Christ Jesus to do good works, which God prepared in advance for us to do.[9]

Sometimes people choose a job to impress their parents, friends or others. Sometimes people choose a career for status or power. After a while they might hate their job because it was the approval of others and the status that attracted them. Knowing that we are all equally valuable in the eyes of God regardless of our chosen career will help. A housewife or househusband does an incredible job looking after the everyday household chores and it is in no way less important work than what a doctor or a pilot or a priest does. In fact, in relation to careers, we need carpenters, plumbers, engineers, cleaners, accountants, paramedics, artists, communication experts and people of all professions for society to function effectively. If everyone becomes a solicitor or business manager who would do the teaching in schools or nursing in hospitals and so on. We need people of all types of careers and skills.

I recently read a book by Oby Bamidele[10] in which the author explains how she worked hard and became an accountant just to get her parents' approval. She struggled in her job because deep down she wanted to be someone who empowers others. With the help of God and her husband, after many years of struggle, she finally fulfilled her dream of becoming a counselor. The argument she makes in her book is that she earned much less as a counselor but was much happier.

We need to enjoy what we do to keep going. A few weeks ago, I preached at a neighboring church. At the end of the service one person came and told me, "I can see that you believe in what you do for the Lord." I thought that summed it all up. The lady might not even remember what I preached but she caught the main thing. When we enjoy what we do and remember that we do it for the glory of God and in the service of God's people, the results will be far-reaching. And whatever career you choose or have chosen you can dedicate it to honor God. Despite the work you do, there is a joy in dedicating your career life to God.

Why do you want to do what you want to do?

If you are deciding on a career path or planning to change your job it might be worth asking why you want to do what you want to do. This will help clarify things in your own mind. It is worth putting your passion clearly into words. Below are the things you can ponder over when you contemplate passion.

P – Pleasing God. How will the career path you choose please God? Is the passion in your heart something that God put there? You might ask how you know. This is how to find out. If your passion is just and righteous and will enhance peace, rebuild people's lives or nurture life on earth, it is possible that God has put it in your heart. If your passion is something that is selfish or if it is something that destroys life and hurts people or yourself it is not a God-inspired passion.

A – Ambition. Know what your ambition is. What do you dream about? Is that ambition put into your heart by God? Letting go of selfish ambitions to follow God's ambition for you might be hard but it will prove to be the right thing. Believe that God's plan for your life is much better than your plan for your life.

S – Skills. When you listen to the ambitions God puts into your heart and mind, He will equip you with the skills needed. Sooner or later God gives you the abilities you need. With God's help you can develop your skills. It is also worth asking what your innate skills and talents are.[11] What are the God-given strengths in you? You might find your call in using them for God, others and yourself.

S – Seriousness. What are you serious about? How will your serious work change the lives of people for the better? Also, how serious are you to change yourself for the better? Often God gives us thoughts. Different things might interest you in life. It is important to pay attention to and pursue the things you love and have a passion for. For example, if you are passionate about seeing people healed you might want to become a kind and caring doctor, or nurse, pharmacist or paramedic. If you love the minute ways a computer works you might want to become a software engineer. If you love crops and plants, you might enjoy being an agriculture officer or farmer. Earning enough money is important but when you enjoy what you do for a living it becomes a blessing. However, God looks at our hearts more than the good work we do. There are numerous ways we could earn our living. God is keener to see our hearts turned towards Him. God-led life is about asking God to be at the center of what we do and what He wants us to do in the future.

I – Interest. You can keep going only when you are interested in something. Many things are easy to start with but when the work gets harder people are generally tempted to quit and give up. For example, if you don't have a keen interest in animals the chances are you won't be a good veterinary doctor or veterinary nurse. If you are not interested in numbers maybe accountancy is not for you. On the other hand, if you have a keen interest in animals you might want to train to be a veterinary nurse or veterinary doctor. If you have a keen interest in building you might want to work towards becoming a builder or a civil engineer or an architect.

O – Overflow. Where and how can your joy overflow? If you are struggling to understand what kind of a person you are or where your joy can overflow, it might be worth taking the Myers Briggs test or another personality test. Knowing how you are wired can help in choosing your career path.

N – No to negativity. When you decide to work with passion, honesty and integrity you may have to surmount obstacles in your path. Questions like "Am I good enough?" or "Can I do it?" or "Does God really want me to do this?" are not uncommon. Believe that God has called you to do what he has put in your heart and that He is there within you and all around you through His Holy Spirit to carry you through.

Hard work – no pain no gain

Many things in life don't have a secret ingredient. It is about persistence, perseverance and hard work. Persistence, perseverance and hard work are absolutely essential in building any career.

Also, it is helpful to remember that with God you can keep going.

Whatever you do, do it for God's glory

Ultimately, the real question is not so much what we want to do with our life but what God wants us to do with our life. As we have seen in the last chapter, when we are connected with God, in and through prayer, you and I are instruments in God's hands. Even a blunt instrument is sharper than the sharpest one when it is in the hands of God. It is God who puts us in the right place before the right people at the right time. If you are a student, it is God who gives you wisdom, memory and understanding. It is God who helps us in workplaces. What is crucial is to stick with God. When we cling on to God our paths become clear, our joy will overflow and we begin to live life with renewed focus and purpose. There is nothing else that can revitalize our life more than dedicating ourselves again and again to live a God-inspired life.

When we live a life connected with God even when we fail, we don't panic too much because we have the confidence that He will take even our failures and turn them into triumphs. Everybody fails at one point or another. However, when we commit our career to God's glory, He is always there to lift us up when we fall or fail.

The key is to get in tune with the "heart" and "mind" of God. Then things will fall into place. Clarity will come in times of confusion. And in times when negative things happen, God will use them in a positive way.

Being God-filled in work places

God calls us to swim against the flow. The values of the fallen world are flesh, corruption and selfishness. Strong and healthy fish are capable of swimming against the flow and they do.

In conclusion, our call in life is much deeper and more profound than our work. It is much more than our career, bank balance, the car we drive or how many bedrooms we have in our house. It is about seeking God, putting our trust in God, constantly renewing our relationship with God and becoming a disciple of God in Jesus. We will look at these in the next sub-chapters.

Questions for reflection or discussion

1. Do you think our character is more important to God than our career?
2. How would you help a teenager struggling to choose her or his career path?
3. How do you overcome negativity and unhealthy competitions in workplaces?
4. Why is it important to know not just your strengths but

also your limitations?

5. Why is working smartly better than looking to cut corners?

6. How does God bless our work when we dedicate it to Him?

3.3 Created for God-inspired discipleship

The World Hates the Disciples. Jesus said, "If the world hates you, keep in mind that it hated me first. If you belonged to the world, it would love you as its own. As it is, you do not belong to the world, but I have chosen you out of the world. That is why the world hates you."[12]

We explored God's purposes for us in relation to our work life in the last sub-chapter. In this section, we will look at our call to discipleship. Discipleship begins by acknowledging that God is Holy, all powerful, He knows better and by humbly and simply submitting yourself to Him.

The call to be a disciple of God in Jesus is a privilege and a joy. God calls us not because we deserve it but because He is gracious and merciful. Everyone is called to be a disciple. We are, in fact, created for a God-inspired discipleship.

Jesus said to Matthew, follow me, and he followed him. Professionally, Matthew was a tax collector. Tax collectors, in Jesus' time, were marginalized and hated in their local communities. They were hated for two reasons. First, they collected tax for the Roman government. Second, they typically loved money more than people. They usually collected more than required and thus they were corrupt. There were no spreadsheets, Microsoft Excel and HMRC as we have today.

So, Matthew's focus had been on how to make more money and become richer every year.

Jesus, who said that he came for sinners and tax collectors

and not for the self-righteous ones, came to Matthew. Jesus said to him, "Follow me." Similar to the other disciples who couldn't resist their call, Matthew couldn't resist the call.

Here is the point. Matthew left what he was after or, more precisely, the money he worshipped and followed Jesus. He became rich but in a different way – earlier he had money but now he had Jesus.

Matthew became a disciple of Jesus. There was no turning back to dishonesty and greed anymore. Perhaps, even though he had enough money, somehow, he knew that he was carrying a heavy load in his heart. As we are relieved when we place our baggage on an airport trolley, Matthew left his burden and traveled with a light heart. He learned from Jesus and lived differently.

I use Matthew here only as an example. All disciples of Jesus had to let go of something as they began to follow Him.

What could this mean for us? In and through the call of Matthew and all the other disciples – Jesus invites you and me to follow Him today. The call is to look at the holiness, splendor and the eternal love of God in Jesus and realize it is worth following Him.

The amazing message here is clear. Our past doesn't matter. And disciples now and then fail too. Peter denied, Thomas doubted, James and John were full of selfishness and pride. But with Jesus their lives changed again and again for the better. Paul, who persecuted the church, started building the church. Jesus, who could change water into wine, can change lives too. With Jesus, it is not about our past. It is about repentance, listening to the call of Jesus and responding to that call just as Matthew and others did.

Jesus wants us to have the heart of a true disciple – ready to commit, ready to repent, ready to listen and ready to obey – knowing that we are sinners in need of forgiveness and redemption. Matthew's story gives us hope that that loving call of Jesus can change our lives for the better.

The same grace which was poured upon Matthew and all the other disciples is pouring upon you even today to bless you and to make you whole.

A disciple is one who listens and learns from Jesus

A disciple is one who abides in Jesus, one who longs to be with him, one who follows him and one who listens to him and obeys him. Like good sheep listen to the shepherd, the disciples listened to Jesus.

Matthew and the other disciples listened and learnt from Jesus. They learnt what it meant to fear God and what it meant to know His presence and obey His commandments. God in Jesus who used Matthew wants to use you and me to join Him in His work. We should not feel unqualified because of our looks or lack of education or lack of confidence. We need to let go of things that hold us back. What God in Jesus looks for is openness, obedience and sincere commitment. Learning from Jesus will reorder our priorities in life and we have to be ready for it. We should also remember that the highest calling in life is to love God and serve Him no matter what the world says.

Disciples live in Christ

A four-year-old child was unwell one day. He asked his father, "Why did I fall sick?" The father replied, "you played in cold water too long and so you have got a high temperature now." The boy took his medication and went to bed. Suddenly, he remembered that his goldfish was in cold water. Thinking that it might fall sick, he jumped out of his bed, went straight to the fish tank and carefully took the fish out of the water. Hearing the noise, the father woke up and found the boy with the fish in his hand. The father asked what he was doing. He replied, "The fish was in the water for too long, it might fall sick." Then his father explained that a fish is meant to live in water. Water is its environment. The boy dropped the fish in the water and it began to swim once again.

Just as a fish is meant to live in water, disciples are meant to live in Christ. There is joy in living in God in Christ.

Jesus prays for His disciples – what more could disciples want

In the prayer of Jesus for the disciples, we find the secret of the joy which disciples need to have. Note that Jesus doesn't pray that they will be great at this and that or they will be famous or popular. His prayer is this, "Father I speak these things in the world so that they may have my joy made complete in themselves."[13]

When the disciples were frightened, the risen Jesus came to them and said, "Peace be with you." They didn't know how He came in but there He was. Jesus came and stood among them. And he said to them, "Peace be with you." Jesus comes into the lives of disciples when they expect Him as well as when they don't expect Him.

What does Jesus pray about for his disciples?

First, Jesus prays that the disciples will live as if they do not belong to this world. He prays, "Father, they do not belong to the world just as I do not belong to the world."

At different points in life, we enter a new world. From being toddlers, children enter into the education world. And when youngsters graduate, they are sent back into a different world – a new world. Then they will be expected to build a career and find a mate, thus separating themselves from their families. And then when people retire, they enter into a new world again.

Discipleship is entering a new and different world. The new world often involves taking risks. It involves accepting hard work and sometimes humiliation and failure. However, the peace of God stays with them and the light of God shines in and through them even in the darkest of times.

Second, disciples are those who work for unity. Jesus prays that they will be "one." Jesus also prays, "Protect them from the evil one." A disciple can rejoice because she/he has God on his/her side.

Third, disciples went out in God's name. They were to travel light. That is simply to say that they had to put their complete trust in God. They had to trust that He would provide. Perhaps, we can add that a person who travels light travels fast and far. If they were not received, they were to shake off the dust from their feet when they left the town. When Rabbis usually entered Palestine after a journey in a Gentile land, they shook off the last particle of heathen dust from their feet. Here, Jesus says that if a village or town doesn't receive you don't worry, shake off the dust from your feet.

Disciples are sent out to proclaim the good news of God in Jesus and His forgiveness through words, deeds and lives.

Fourth, discipleship is about sharing peace. "When you enter a house, first say, 'Peace to this house.' If someone who promotes peace is there, your peace will rest on them; if not, it will return to you."[14]

If people accept, all well and good. Otherwise go to the next village or town. The peace of God never goes to waste. The peace you proclaimed comes back to you. The duty of a disciple is to share the peace and the light they have in Christ with others. These are the things we need.

Discipleship is about proclaiming that the Kingdom of God is near

There is so much pain and suffering in the world. However, Jesus insists that the Kingdom is nearby. If you and I want to be a disciple, we are invited to learn to see how near the Kingdom is. Often the Kingdom is not in the big things we see but in the small things. In England, we talk about St. Paul's Cathedral or

Westminster Abbey or the other bigger churches in the world. Well, God is there. But I know of an elderly lady in her late eighties who lives in a village and there is a small church there. The village church has a worship service there once every two months. Nevertheless, this elderly woman opens the church every morning, lights a candle, spends time in prayer and locks the church in the evening. The Kingdom of God is in big things but also in small things. Disciples are those who have learned to look purposefully beneath the surface and realize what is possible with God despite themselves.

Questions for reflection or discussion

1. What do you think Jesus actually meant when He invited His disciples to "follow Him"?
2. What changes will you have to make if you decide to become a disciple of God in Jesus (or renew your discipleship) today?
3. Do you think being a disciple is a duty or a joy?
4. What, in your opinion, are the tasks of a disciple?
5. We are created for a life of discipleship. However, what are the main obstacles people face today? How do we overcome them?
6. When people see you and listen to you, are there enough signs to reveal that you are a disciple?

3.4 Gentle proclamation and healthy witness

Proclaiming the gospel is one beggar telling another where they found food.
(D.T. Niles)

Every Saint has a past and every sinner has a future.
(Oscar Wilde)

There is a true story of Fritz Kreisler (1875–1962), the famous violinist who earned a lot with his concerts and compositions. Nevertheless, he kindly gave most of it away. One day he discovered a superb violin on one of his trips. But he didn't have enough money to buy it. Later, having raised enough cash to meet the asking price he returned to the seller, hoping to purchase that magnificent instrument. But to his great disappointment it had been sold to a collector.

Kreisler made his way to the new owner's home and offered to buy the violin. The collector said it had become his treasured possession and he would not sell it. Very disheartened, Kreisler was about to leave when he had an idea. "Could I play the instrument once more before it is consigned to silence?" he asked. Permission was granted, and the great virtuoso filled the room with such heart moving music that the collector's emotions were deeply stirred. "I have no right to keep that to myself," he exclaimed. "It's yours, Mr. Kreisler. Take it into the world, and let people hear it."[15]

We, as people who live in communities, generally share our good news and not so good news with our friends and neighbors. This sort of communication is normal and natural. For a believer, the greatest good news is that they have found God and they have experienced their greatest delight in God. Proclamation of this good news is something that is normal and natural. Of course, people need to be gentle, kind, simple, humble, honest and considerate when they share their greatest good news with others. They have to be open to listen to the point of view of others too.

St. Paul talks about the joy of faith and the joy of putting faith into action referring to the example of Abraham. Paul in his letters often takes pleasure in explaining the joy, peace and fulfillment that comes through faith and mission. For him, the joy of faith and witness has no boundaries because God doesn't have boundaries.

In the Book of Romans, Paul explains this using the adventure and patience of Abraham's journey of faith and witness.[16] For Paul, Abraham's faith was the faith that was ready for adventure and witness. He went out not knowing where he was going. His faith was the faith that had patience. When he reached the promised land, he was never allowed to possess it. He had to wander in it, a stranger and a tent-dweller, as his descendants one day were to wander in the wilderness too. To Abraham, God's promises never came fully true until after he died; and yet he never abandoned his faith and witness. The person who trusts in God implicitly, is the person whose hope is bright and whose effort is intensely strenuous. And that is so, even in the days when there is nothing to do but wait. Abraham rejoiced in his faith and that faith gave him a big vision and mission. Faith and action went together for him and he found holiness, peace, purpose and fulfillment in his faith and mission. Abraham remains an example for us, even today.

God calls everyone to proclaim and witness

God called Abraham. He made His covenant with the people who participated in the Abrahamic call. The call to Moses also illustrates God's call. The situation was ripe. The people of Israel were in bondage in Egypt. As with all depressed and oppressed people, the likelihood of a deliverer rising up from within their midst was remote. The Jewish slaves in Egypt needed someone who could understand their distress, and yet at the same time was not bogged down in the despair that paralyzed them. These conditions were met in Moses.

We live in the same world. As King Solomon says, "There is nothing new under the Sun."[17] God who called Abraham, Moses and many others, continues to call you and me today.

God invites us to rejoice in our faith translated into mission and action. So, look out for what God's calling is for you in your church and in your community.

Christian ministry is holistic. There is a story of the British woman who spent some months serving God's people in Kenya. On her final visit to a remote township, she attended the clinic of a medical mission. As the local women there began to sing together, she found herself deeply moved by their beautiful harmonies. She totally committed herself to always remember this sacred and holy moment and was determined to share it with friends when she got home. With tears flowing down her cheeks, she turned to her friend and asked, "Please tell me the meaning of the song?" Her friend looked at her and solemnly said – the meaning is: "If you drink boiled water, you won't get dysentery." After a long pause, the British woman defended herself with a positive note. Every place is God's place and every good work is God's work and that is true.

Taking the cross and following Christ and losing our lives for His sake is to say that our faith should be expressed in our actions and life. What the gospel gives us is the insight that every aspect of life belongs to God. There is no area of practical wisdom that is separate from the wisdom of God. This means that children who study should ask how their study is going to help others. Those of us who work should ask how it is helpful. Jesus came to give us life to the full. The question each one of us must ask is how our daily life fits into God's purposes for good in the world.

Rejoice in proclamation and witness

Humanity looks for joy and gladness. Interestingly, the Bible teaches us that God calls His people to rejoice and be glad in their proclamation of the gospel and witness.

The prophet Isaiah rejoices in witnessing God by bringing God's message to the Israelites. He is an example for us even today. In Isaiah 65, the prophet says that God is in the process of creating everything anew for His people. Indeed, Isaiah rejoices in proclaiming that good news to the Israelites. It is significant that Isaiah not only rejoices but also calls the Israelites to rejoice and to be glad in their proclamation and witness to what God is doing. The climax of the prophet's reason to rejoice and to be glad is found in the final verse of that chapter. For him, God is creating a new earth where the wolf and the lamb shall lie down together and the lion shall eat straw like the ox.

Someone said that the lion and the lamb might lie down together but the lamb might not get enough sleep. It is true that we live in a world where injustice, exploitation and atrocities are quite common. But that is exactly why proclamation and witness about the heavenly kingdom which will be made possible by God is essential. Like Isaiah, we could rejoice in our proclamation of the good news and our witness to God because we join in that prophetic proclamation and witness which is essential even today. A friend of mine and an evangelist once said, "If we cannot rejoice in our proclamation and witness for our Lord, there is a leak in our Christianity somewhere."

If we turn our attention to Paul, we would see him say this. To Timothy he writes, "Share in the sufferings like a good soldier of Jesus Christ."[18] To understand the true meaning of what Paul is trying to tell Timothy we need to know the relationship between Paul and Timothy. Paul calls Timothy, "my beloved child." Apparently, this means Paul loved Timothy just as a father loves his child. Of course, Timothy is not a biological son of Paul but these letters are from a spiritual Father to his beloved spiritual child. Paul says, Timothy, my beloved son, "You share in the sufferings like a good soldier of Jesus Christ."

However, in our day-to-day life we see most living beings taking care of their little ones. The birds fly far to find food for their little ones. The animals provide food, shelter and protect their little ones. Human beings give good education, food, shelter and everything they can to their children. Christian parents pray that their children will know God and put their trust in Him. In short, parents want the best for their children. They want their children to be happy and away from suffering and pain.

On the contrary, Paul calls Timothy my beloved child and tells him to share in the sufferings like a good soldier of Jesus Christ. Is this because Paul didn't really love Timothy? No, not at all. Paul advises Timothy from his own life experience. Paul had two kinds of life. The first lifestyle which he lived was the one before his conversion experience, recorded in Acts chapter 9. Paul was a well-educated person in his society. He learned under Gamaliel, one of the best scholars of his time. Also, Paul was a rich man financially. He was born into an affluent family. Moreover, Paul also held a good position and immense power in the Roman government. In general terms he lived a well-settled and good life. It was with his position, influence and power that he was going to Damascus to persecute Christians. He encountered Christ like a light from heaven and he heard a voice saying, "Why do you persecute me?"

After that experience Paul lived a different kind of life, which he called life in Christ or new life. In fact, it was a life with suffering and pain. During his missionary journeys he faced shipwrecks and he was in the ocean for one full day and night. He was also stoned, beaten, imprisoned and persecuted for preaching the gospel. He says, "Five times I received from the Jews the forty lashes minus one,"[19] for preaching and witnessing.

Obviously, Paul loved his second way of life in which he suffered for the gospel of Christ. He found more happiness, blessing, supreme joy and his purpose fulfilled when he lived for Christ and people of God.

That is why he tells Timothy to share in the suffering like a good soldier of Jesus Christ. Though it was a life of suffering for Christ, Paul had something great – that great joy in his heart – which he lacked in his first way of life. The peace, the joy, the hope and happiness and the abundant life which he had because of Christ's presence with him surpassed the pain of all the sufferings he underwent.

The final teaching of Jesus

Notably, proclamation and witness were the last messages from
Jesus to His listeners. On the day of ascension, Jesus told His
disciples that it is not important for them to know the times that
God has set by divine authority. But what is important for them
to know is that they will be His witnesses in Jerusalem, in all
Judea and Samaria and to the ends of the earth, which includes
where you and I are right now.

I have seen a beautiful picture of Jesus' ascension. In that
picture, Jesus is rising up as the disciples watch him in awe
with their mouths wide open. But soon my attention was drawn
to the ground, where the artist painted the footsteps of Jesus.
Most probably, the painter is pressing the viewers with the old
question, "Why do you stand looking up into heaven? Look at
these footprints here on the earth." Bearing witness could mean
continuing to walk in the footsteps of Christ.

Prior to His ascension, Jesus also said to his disciples that
they will be His witnesses when the Holy Spirit comes upon
them. And on the day of Pentecost the spirit of God descended
upon His church. And God's spirit is with God's people always.

We will rejoice in bearing witness when we experience and
understand God, not as a projection out there but as the root
of our very being. When we realize that God never leaves His
people alone, we cannot but rejoice in bearing witness to him.

Today some in our society ask whether doing good work isn't
enough to bear witness to God. Of course, it is good if we do
good works. But it is better if we also tell one another who has
sent us to do the good works we do. Jesus bore witness to God
the Father throughout his life.

As you read this, my prayer is that God will encourage you
to consider making a little progress in your witness. You could
decide to have a family prayer time or a personal prayer time,

if you don't do that already, by cutting down a little time from watching TV. Or you could decide that you will share your experience of God with one of your friends this week. Or you may decide to be a bit friendlier with your colleagues and family members. Witness is all about letting others know what God has done for you, is doing for you and will do for you. Witnessing is our privilege, our purpose, our joy and our way towards oneness with God.

Mother Teresa visited Cambridge in 1976 to give a talk at the University there. The fragile body of the Albanian nun climbed up the platform to rapturous applause. When the clapping was over, she said, "In the West, one of the greatest problems is loneliness. People die alone. You have the greatest evidence of poverty. Poverty of the spirit. It can be fed only by the bread of heaven: Jesus Christ. In India, our greatest problem is togetherness. Diseases are easily shared but hardly anyone dies alone. We have the greatest evidence of poverty. Physical poverty. It can be fed only by the bread of heaven: Jesus Christ."[20]

Then she took out a loaf of bread from her bag – broke it in half, passed it on and asked them to share it with joy, and go and do likewise.

Most helpfully, Jesus not only teaches us but also in Jesus we see our model. Following Jesus, we should never be afraid to take the lead and stand up for truths that are countercultural. At the same time this is the servant leadership modeled by God in Christ who took the towel and washed His disciples' feet. It takes patience and it takes sacrifice and it takes commitment to live a God-inspired life.

To conclude this sub-chapter, like Moses, Abraham, Paul and millions of others, may the Lord give us a faith which is ready for exploration. A faith which is ready for proclamation and witness. A faith which is also looking beyond this world. A faith which believes the incredible, and therefore makes it possible for us to be sojourners and strangers, for our true home is in God.

We now move on to explore God's purposes for us in terms of our fruitful living and mission in the final section of this chapter.

Questions for reflection or discussion

1. How important do you think sharing the gospel is? And why?
2. Do you think actions speak more powerfully than words? Reflect or discuss.
3. How could your daily life fit into God's purposes for good in the world?
4. What opportunities do you have for gentle evangelism and healthy witness in your community?
5. What is the one change you can make in your life to live a life of witness?
6. Can you name one or two people who have helped you in your faith journey?

3.5 Fruitfulness, mission and service

Do all the good you can, by all the means you can, in all the ways you can, in all the places you can, at all the times you can, to all the people you can, as long as you can…. That is greatness.
(John Wesley)

The scripture teaches us that we are created to live a fruitful life. How do we do this? We have to make a decision. The choice with life is this: we can live however we like and however we want to live. We can spend our time, money and talents in our own ways. Alternatively, we can invite God into our lives and ask Him to help us live a life of fruitfulness, mission and service.

According to St. Paul, these are the choices. One choice is to have bad fruits. On the one hand, the bad fruits we can have in our life are – fornication, impurity, licentiousness, idolatry (putting anything else before God is idolatry), sorcery, enmities, strife (creating conflict – trouble maker), jealously, anger, quarrels, dissensions (rebellion), factions (divisions), envy, drunkenness and things like these.[21]

On the other hand, we can live with Love – agape love, joy (the joy that comes from God), peace, patience, kindness, generosity, faithfulness, gentleness and self-control.[22]

If I show you a bowl of rotten, smelly, spoiled fruits and if I show you some good fresh aromatic – delightful fruits – which one would you choose. Obviously, the good ones.

Similarly, God looks at us and he sees what kind of fruits we have in our lives. Do we want to live with good fruits or not so good fruits? If we look at our past life – and if we are honest – it might not have been all good. Nonetheless, God is forgiving when we ask for it and He invites us to be confident and bear good fruits from now on.

And that doesn't mean we will not get things wrong again. But His grace is there to help us start again. When we make a mess of our life or even when we make a mess at church or other places, He helps us start again because that's what God does. He never gives up on us, which is indeed encouraging.

Mission and service as joy and life

Jesus once said, "If any want to follow me, let them deny themselves, take up their cross and follow me."[23] In other words, if any want to follow me let them take pain and suffering for the sake of my mission and follow me. Then he went on to say, "For those who save their life will lose it, and those who lose their life for my sake will find it." Now, you might ask, Jesus talks about pain and the cross and where is the life and joy in it? In fact, to understand these words of Jesus we need to know the paradoxical style of his teaching. Jesus again and again revealed that he is a teacher of paradox. For example, He says that blessed are the poor (in our worldly terms both blessed and poor don't go together) but for Him, theirs is the kingdom of God. Then He says that the humble ones will be exalted and those who exalt themselves will be humbled. Yet another time, He says that the first will be last and the last will be first. In a similar manner, He says that those who lose (let go) their life for His sake will find life. For Him, true joy and true life are to be found in taking pain and struggle for God and others.

The popularity time of Jesus was coming to an end. Jesus realized that it was time for his journey towards Jerusalem, towards the cross. Hence, He began to teach His disciples the most important things that He wanted to teach them. It is in this situation He says to them that those who lose their life for His sake will find life and those who want to become His followers, let them deny themselves, take up their cross and follow Him.

For Jesus, true joy and life in its fullness should be found not in avoiding suffering for his sake or for the sake of His mission, but in taking it. Interestingly, even though the disciples had now lived with Jesus for more than three years they didn't understand where to find true life and true joy. They were ready to be chief ministers in the government that Jesus would establish. They were ready to sit at His right side and left side. All their hopes were lost when He said, "Lose your life for my sake and you will find it." Jesus gave them an ad hoc lecture in God's economic plan quite contrary to their expectations. In fact, a life that is spent soothing the pain of the hurt, caring for children in need, hammering nails in houses for those without shelter, sharing bread with the hungry, visiting those in prison, and denying oneself may be like a squandered or foolish life in the economy of a self-centered age, but in the storehouse of Christ it is an extravagant treasure. Life and joy are to be found in mission and service.

The saints of God found joy and abundant life in helping others, visiting the sick, listening to those in pain, taking the gospel to the most difficult places and taking pain for others. I have read of a British missionary who came to India and worked for leprosy patients. Every day he visited them, cleaned their wounds, fed them and preached the good news of Christ to them. Eventually, working very close with them, he himself became a leprosy patient and later died of leprosy. It is told that before he died, he whispered, "I once said that Jesus loves *you* even lepers. But now I rejoice in saying that Jesus loves *us* even lepers." Such was his commitment and dedication. Such was the joy and life that most missionaries found in participating in God's mission. Another missionary was asked by a Hindu, "Why do you work so hard? Is it to go to heaven?" He replied, "No, I don't work hard to go to heaven. But my participation in Christ's mission itself brings me the greatest joy." Then he added, "If I go to heaven, I might not be content with the luxury in heaven. I will request God to send me as a missionary to hell." Here I should add that all these missionaries were not full-time priests or ministers. Some were doctors, others engineers, others teachers, yet others nurses, linguists, artists, retired people and so on. But they manifested the love of Christ in whatever they did.

These people of God and many others understood what Jesus meant by saying take your cross and follow me. They understood that true joy and life are to be found in losing life for Christ's sake and the sake of His people. All those who accumulated millions did not find where true joy and life is. All those who became celebrities did not find where true joy and life is. Even kings like Solomon who had a thousand wives said it is in vain. Then, who were the people who understood where true joy and life was? It was those who found joy and life in helping others. It was those who lost their lives for the sake of His mission.

Where do you find your greatest joy and abundant life? You might be doing good work in your church and society. You might be helping a person in need or you might be working for a charity. The good news to you today is – don't just do the good work that you do but rejoice in the good work that you do.

Why? Because Jesus says that when you lose your life for His sake you are really finding life. Temporary happiness might be found in many places but true joy or sustainable bliss and life in its fullness are to be found in our involvement in God's on-going mission.

Very practically, in addition to all that you do, consider doing one more good work this week/month if these words of Christ speak to you today. It might be just saying the words "I love you" to a parent, sister or brother with whom you have not kept in touch, or it might be doing a small good deed to someone in need.

The disciples eventually understood the paradox of Jesus' teaching. They didn't understand it when Jesus said, "Lose your life to save it." However, they fully understood it when they saw the cross and then the risen Jesus. Earlier, Peter said that no suffering should come upon Jesus but now he has learned. Now he is fully prepared to suffer for the gospel, mission and service. The disciples went out with abundant joy and abundant life to be the feet, hands, heart and mouth of Jesus. Jesus who taught his disciples tells us even as you read this to find your purpose in seeking true joy and true life in being His feet, hands, heart and mouth. It is for the Christian faith that Jesus lost his life so that we may have life and have it abundantly. He will be delighted when we lose our life for His sake and for the sake of His mission so that we may find our new life and true joy in Him now and for all eternity.

Mission and service of people in the past

The Good Samaritan story is spoken about often. Although the Bible calls him Samaritan[24] the whole world today knows him as the "Good" Samaritan. You and I are created by God to be good Samaritans drawing from the example of the faithful people who have lived before our time.

We see in history that the faithful have the longing to devote themselves to common good. Mission and service-oriented people have founded schools, universities, and hospitals (in many countries hospitals are run by churches alongside the government). In the UK, we can find the following founded by inspired Christians: cooperatives, housing associations, building societies, common investment funds, industrial and provident and friendly societies, benevolent societies, museums, informal community organizations, parent-teacher associations, credit unions and the innumerable charities like Samaritans, Tear Fund, Christian Aid, Water Aid, USPG, Amnesty International and so on. These remain an inspiration for us today.

The world we live in is also inhabited by the lost. We need to help each other for God's mission to be complete. Mission-minded people have played an enormous role in helping others. It is here worth noting that mission-minded nuns and chaplains have through their work provided many a prisoner with their Damascus Road experience. People can change, but they need the inspiration in great measure to do so. And it is our belief that there is no greater power to change lives than faith, than the presence of God's spirit, and through an encounter with Jesus, in His life, death and resurrection.

Moreover, there is a joy in faith because faith is what brings anyone in communion with God. God made us because His joy boiled over, and that's what we are made for, and when we strive to find that receptivity to the bare reality of God, then actually what it's about is joy, at the end of the day. It is when we understand this, we begin to enjoy God and live for Him.

That is why the church talks about the great saints, not just as the super-achievers of the church's history but as an illustration of what the life of people with faith can make possible; they are a series of vignettes of people who rejoiced in God. Faith transformed them completely. Faith should affect all of us as well as all of each of us, every bit of every person.

St. Aelred said that our hearts are like "a spiritual Noah's

Ark" made of imperishable wood or virtues and good deeds. In the spiritual ark of our hearts, we should gather and care for all those who are in any kind of need, particularly those likely to drown in the chaos of their lives. Now, it would be wonderful if each one of us could take that image and make it a reality in our lives and in the lives of others.

Imagine if our hearts were a spiritual Noah's Ark for all those who are unloved, frightened, lost and in need in our world today, and we invite God to be with us in that ark. He is faithful. He keeps His promises. He helps us to be focused, fruitful and draw closer to His kingdom day by day. In conclusion, we all have to make a choice. God-inspired life is to live fruitfully and to make mission and service a part of our life.

In the next chapter, we will devote ourselves to learn ways in which we can overcome temptations and trials. This is an important dimension that we need to explore as we seek to live a God-inspired life. Living out God's purposes for us includes receiving forgiveness and holy living – overcoming ungodly distractions. We now move on to analyze this dimension in life.

Questions for reflection or discussion

1. Have you experienced the joy of making sacrifices so that others might have a better life? Can you give one example?
2. Does the exemplary life of the saints of the past centuries inspire you?
3. What is the one thing you could do to bring the light of God in to your church or community?
4. What is the mission concern God has put in your thoughts?
5. God liberates His people for His mission. What is the liberation you would like God to bring to you today?
6. Often great things have small beginnings. Do you sense God calling you for any particular ministry?

Chapter 4

Life Is a Test —
God-Inspired Life Is to Win the Test

4.1 Know that you are so precious to God

For I am the LORD your God who takes hold of your right hand and says to you, Do not fear; I will help you.[1]

Obstacles are the frightful things you see when you take your eyes off your goal.
(Henry Ford)

Trials and temptations are part of life. No one is exempt from them. This is a dimension in life that we explore in this chapter. We are too precious, in God's eyes, to give in to ungodly distractions. In fact, we can overcome temptations with the help of God. Crucially, we can also receive forgiveness from God in Christ for our past sins and guilt when we repent and pray for it with an earnest and contrite heart.

Nothing worth doing is easy in this world. If you want to do well in any aspect of your life, there are obstacles you need to overcome. It is when you are determined, focused and resilient that you get there in the end. An athlete doesn't become a champion overnight. There are many hurdles to overcome. There is so much hard work to do. A musician practices for many years on end before performing in public. People who are resilient do not give up or give in and they know that failures are part of the process that eventually leads to success. Similarly, there are obstacles we need to overcome so that we can live a God-inspired life. What is encouraging is that, as the prophet Isaiah writes, God is the one who takes hold of our hand and leads us in the journey of life.

The test in our life centers around making choices and the right ones at that. The Book of Genesis as well as other books in Scripture portray that we need to make the right choices with the help of God. However, there come occasions in life when we feel that we are not good enough to be faithful people of God. Here we will see how to tackle this.

Feeling not good enough

We might feel that we are not good enough. In one sense it is true that no one is good except God. As St. Paul would say everyone, has fallen short of God's glory.[2] Jesus Himself said, "No one is good but God alone."[3]

However, God doesn't want us to keep thinking that we are not good enough and give up. These biblical verses teach us to rely on God's goodness and strength rather than our own. If we keep thinking that we are not good enough for God, we might ignore God and live our lives in our way rather than live the life God intends us to live. If we give in to the feeling of being not good enough, we will miss out on the confidence, peace, light and fulfillment which a God-inspired life brings to us.

The truth is that Jesus gave Himself for us on the cross and rose again for us. When we bring before God the things that make us feel "not good enough," He replenishes and fortifies us and makes us more than "good enough" and gives us positive thoughts that reassure us. Also, the fact is that we aim to live a God-led life not because we are good enough but because God is good and He is good enough to make you and me good enough.

Even many biblical giants didn't feel good enough. Moses didn't feel good enough. Gideon didn't feel good enough. Samuel didn't feel that David, the shepherd, was good enough. Mary didn't feel good enough, Zacchaeus didn't feel good enough and none of the disciples felt good enough. It becomes evident from the fact that they all ran away or denied or doubted themselves.

All we need to do is to seek God's help and trust that in His eyes you and I are good enough to live a life inspired by God. It is He who makes us good enough and that's what matters.

God in Christ is a God who restores

We live in a world where people often wear masks to protect themselves and their identity. Sadly, many also wear masks because they are afraid to be themselves. Here we can look at Peter as an example. Peter had followed Jesus for about three and half years. He learned a lot from Jesus and he knew that he was called to be a faithful disciple. Nonetheless, the day before Jesus was crucified, he put on a "mask." He had to disguise himself. A servant girl said, "This man is a Galilean and this man has been with Jesus." Peter denied his identity. He wore the mask of a foreigner. He said, "I don't know him at all. Who is this you are talking about?" He continued to live behind that mask even after Jesus' crucifixion. He needed a mask to hide his identity and deny Jesus. And later he needed another mask to hide his guilt, shame and sin.

In fact, after the resurrection Jesus came to Peter to tear off his mask and to free him from his disguise. Peter's story is the story of many people. Today, the Peter behind a mask might be you and me. Peter's story, thankfully, is a story of grace, of love and of renewal and restoration.

In John's Gospel, we read that after Andrew tells Simon that they have found the Messiah, Jesus sees Simon and renames him "Peter," which means rock.[4] Jesus told him to become a fisherman of people. Then Peter tried to walk on water with the help of Jesus and he went up the mountain and experienced the event of Jesus' transfiguration. Peter also had a mouth that worked for Jesus –well, most of the time. Peter said that Jesus was the Messiah and he so loved him that he did not want him to die. Then one day he was incredibly frightened, he opened his mouth thrice to deny Jesus. It is on that day he started hiding behind his mask. Peter's own confidence and strength dried up.

He knew that he was sand, not "the rock." That's why he went outside to weep after his denial. He ran away because he knew who he was. He knew he was a sinner living with shame and guilt. A sinner in need of cleansing and forgiveness! A sinner in need of being emptied of his sin, guilt and shame!

In fact, we all need emptying, cleansing, forgiveness and new life. The great news is God in Jesus cleanses us and is eager to dwell in us as temples of God. We are created so that God can dwell in us. He readily empties us and cleanses us when we seek His help. He also helps us to overcome obstacles in our lives.

Peter's entire life – what he thought, spoke and did, centered around Jesus and His love for humanity. He emptied himself so much so that he needed to rely on his Lord and savior to be in his life. He wanted the assurance that Jesus indeed rose from the dead. On being told that the grave in which Jesus was buried was found to be empty on Easter morning, Peter ran to the tomb. He, too, found the tomb empty. Still the immense significance of this did not strike him. He did not view or accept it as an event with transformative power. He decided to return to his traditional occupation of fishing and he did. Not only that he caught no fish, he felt a sense of despondency. From the biblical story we can gauge that Peter might have felt a sense of failure and awfulness. Even as time went by, nothing good was coming his way.

The moral of the story is that we could fail like Peter. However, God has a plan for His people and rebuilds their lives.

Peter went fishing again. While fishing he heard a voice calling out to him and his friends from the shore. The man on the shore said, "Friends, throw your net on the other side."[5] They did as they were told and caught plenty. It was then John figured out that it was Jesus Himself. It was at that point that Peter could not hold back anymore. He jumped out of the boat and came to Jesus. Now his mask was beginning to fall away but still neither spoke. Peter was probably unable to talk or, even to approach the one he'd run away from, the one he'd denied.

Peter needed Jesus to graciously reach out to him, not to confront or rebuke him. Peter needed Jesus to forgive him, to help him remove his disguise and to rehabilitate him, to make him new again and again and again.

Jesus turned to Peter and asked him, Simon, son of John, "Do you truly love me?" He said, "Yes." He asked the second time, "Do you love me?" He said, "Yes." And the third time Jesus asked, "Do you love me?" Peter got hurt, when Jesus asked him the third time.[6] And it was at this point that the mask completely went. He may have wept again. The voice of Jesus made him whole again. It changed him. He said, "Lord, you know everything, you know that I love you." Jesus didn't swear at him or tell him off but gently reached out to this wounded, hurt, guilt-filled Peter. God in Christ emptied Peter and re-filled him with Himself, His Spirit. He renewed His relationship with Peter. Healing took place. His mask was torn off and his disguise was removed. He was then prepared to proclaim boldly that he was a Galilean and that he was with Jesus. Jesus restored a hurt person and healed a wounded soul.

If Peter was to grow and become the rock that Jesus said he was to be, Jesus had to re-commission him; call him again. So, Jesus asked Peter if he loved him. His responses empowered Peter to return to ministry. He needed the words of Christ – Feed my lambs. Tend my sheep. Feed my sheep. Peter was to minister to the flock, to those who heard Jesus' voice and to the ones who were willing to listen to it.

We can assume that Jesus asked the question three times because Peter denied Him thrice. I think that the mask on his face had become an almost permanent fixture so Jesus had to ask three times to make sure it was no longer there. Peter was being re-assured of the calling Christ invested in him. Jesus renewed and restored in him the authority to teach and preach. This is good news for us as well. Restoration was then necessary for

Peter. Restoration is now necessary for all of us. It is available for all who seek it from God in Jesus.

Peter knew that he must not look to himself for his strength and abilities but had to look to Jesus for help and direction. Jesus called Peter again and said, "follow me." Earlier he couldn't follow Jesus unto the cross but now he was ready to walk that same road.

Peter boldly preached to thousands and three thousand people were "converted" in one day. Earlier, Peter fell apart when questioned by a servant girl. Once he had become a changed man in Christ, he was able to face an unknown crowd in Jerusalem, unafraid and not on his own, through the power of the Holy Spirit.

Tradition says that Peter later endured persecution but, he didn't deny any more. Amidst all the stumbles and falls, which continued throughout his life, the name the Master had given him, "Rock," became reality.

God's grace that flowed abundantly on that seaside beach is with us always to tear away our masks and make us whole again.

Sometimes we wear metaphorical masks to give the impression that everything in our life is rosy and perfect. But we need to stop and think if we are following Jesus and obeying His call. If not, what is stopping us? Jesus took up the cross for Peter and for you and me. His grace flows into us tearing away our masks. By His grace we become a forgiven and healed people. He invites you and me to live differently, to live as witnesses to Him.

Do you love me? Let us respond by saying – Lord you know everything; you know that I love you.

In our personal lives, do we live behind masks? It is sometimes painful to live behind masks with our personal problems, worries, guilt, failures or whatever it may be but, the voice of Christ makes us whole. Today through this story of Peter, God tells us – feed my lambs, tend my sheep, feed my sheep. Living the gospel is the way of the cross, but it is also where meaning of life, purpose of life, fullness of life and real joy is.

God invites us to live differently, without the masks we put on ourselves. We might fail again and again but He restores and renews.

I meet many people who carry sin, guilt and shame. These are heavy loads to carry. Peter's story is a story of motivation to empty ourselves of the loads that we don't need to carry. Instead, we are called to know that we are made in God's image. You and I are so precious and valuable to God that we are justified in believing that He cares for us. We are forgiven sinners, blessed enough to undertake the sojourn without heavy loads or the burden of personal, spiritual and social baggage. When we ask for it in prayer, God in Christ offers forgiveness and lifts the burden of past sins and guilt, which we carry in our hearts. Jesus went to the cross for us so that we can be set free of any heavy loads we carry. In conclusion, in this section we gained inspiration to live a godly life from the example of Peter. In the next sub-chapter, we will explore lessons from three parables about faithful living.

Questions for reflection and discussion

1. Resilience is important to keep going in life. How can we grow our resilience?
2. How would you respond to a friend who says, "I feel I am not good enough"?
3. What are the masks which people generally wear to disguise themselves today?
4. How do you cope with failures? What helps you to let go of failures?
5. How can God bring restoration and healing in our lives? What would reaffirm you that you are precious to God?
6. Which aspect of Peter's story do you find inspiring? And why?

4.2 It is not about living successfully but faithfully: Lessons from three parables

Personal success or personal satisfaction are not worth another thought if one does achieve them, or worth worrying about if they evade one or are slow in coming. All that is really worthwhile is action –
faithful action, for the world, and in God.
(Pierre Teilhard de Chardin)

I know, my God, that you test the heart and have pleasure in uprightness.[7]

God loves a faithful heart

Having learned in the previous sub-chapter that we are precious to God and thereby we ought to live a godly life, we now move on to reflect on faithful living which pleases God.

Jesus was an admirable storyteller. Jesus told stories which had a lesson. He wanted to teach the truth about God and His Kingdom using simple examples from the day-to-day lives of people. He wanted people to live faithfully everyday despite the failures or successes they faced in life.

One day, Jesus was in Capernaum and some people there came to Him to listen to His stories. They really loved his stories because he used down-to-earth language. He told stories about donkeys, camels, sheep, seeds and soil. Usually, Jesus would tell stories about the common things of life and then at the end of the story, He would often leave them with a conundrum. And then the people would go home and try to figure it out.

"The sower and the seeds" is one of those stories.[8] A sower went to sow seeds. As he sowed seeds, some seeds fell on the path. The birds ate them up. Some seeds fell on rocky ground. Those seeds grew but soon they died because they couldn't stand the heat of the sun. Some other seeds fell among thorns and the thorns grew up and choked them. But some seeds fell on good soil and brought forth grain, some a hundredfold, some sixtyfold and some thirtyfold.

People couldn't understand this story and so they asked what it meant. Jesus was really asking why so much goodness is produced in some people's lives and not in others? Why is it that some people produce and glow with a life of love, peace, patience, kindness, gentleness, faithfulness and self-control? Why is it that some Christians have a hundred fruits of love, benevolence and goodness? Why is that? This is the underlying question of this parable.

Jesus continued to explain His story. He said that some people, sadly, have hardened hearts. Their hearts are hard towards God. God's word doesn't get to their hardened hearts. Some people have shallow hearts. The seeds in their hearts grow very quickly. But when suffering comes, they just die. We know that some trees look strong but when the wind blows they fall down because their roots are not deep and strong. Some people have other priorities in their hearts rather than God. The seeds in their hearts grow but the worldly short time pleasures choke the fruits of the spirit in them

Nonetheless, some seeds fell on good soil. They fell on faithful hearts. They grew because those hearts longed for the seeds to sprout and to grow and to yield good fruits. They yielded a hundredfold, sixtyfold and thirtyfold.

Good soil is a must. A faithful heart is a necessity to live a God-inspired life. It takes time, prayer, patience and perseverance to yield good fruits. Are we faithful in cultivating the soil of our heart diligently? It is not about being successful all the time. It is also not about giving up when we fail. It is about being faithful to God.

Just as an owner of a field feels happy to see one's crops yielding a good harvest full of fruits, God will be pleased with us when our hearts remain faithful to Him.

We have the potential to be faithful but only with God's help

Jesus talks about you and me being wheat or weed in another parable. A good farmer sows wheat which has the potential to produce more wheat. A good God created you and me and so we have the potential to be faithful. However, the truth is all of us have a bit of wheat and a bit of weed in us. The great news is that, with God's help, we can change and become more Christ-like which is to say to become more wheat-like.

Matthew records the parable of wheat and weed.[9] This parable says that there are the godly-ones and the not-so-godly-ones in this world. In fact, one day a person could be wheat and the next day s/he could be weed.

A casual reading of this parable may lead us to consider the world and conclude – Oh yes, that is correct! On the one hand, there are the saintly, the kind-hearted, the committed and the faithful people and on the other hand, there are the evil ones in this world. Further, this parable says that God alone can rightly judge anyone. Of course, an objective analysis of this passage is important.

However, a subjective understanding of this parable will reveal a much deeper layer of meaning to us. In fact, this parable calls us to re-think and re-assess ourselves using the question: Are we being like the wheat or like the weed in this world?

Interestingly, the weed doesn't necessarily destroy the wheat. We may say that the weed is bad because it takes the water, space and nutrients away from the wheat. But all these things, which the weed does, become negative because they are not faithful to the farmer.

The wheat, we know yields fruit, which is made into bread. Jesus says that people who live like the wheat are children of the kingdom. The wheat gives life to those who feed on it. It gives sustenance.

Notably, this parable shows that we can either be like the wheat or like the weed. There is no stance in between. Sometimes we decide to commit our entire life to God but are tempted to keep some parts of it to ourselves. If we decide to keep some parts of our life for selfish interest, there is the danger of ruining our entire life.

Nevertheless, we need not dwell on the idea of divine wrath that is implicit in this parable. During the days of Julian of Norwich, in the fourteenth century, people were terrified of divine wrath. Interpreting passages like these, churches had emphasized divine judgment – i.e., the weed will be burnt in fire. Knowing that becoming preoccupied with one's fallenness can be psychologically corrosive, Julian helpfully said that God's love for the good that we want to do is most important to God.

In fact, just as the owner of a piece of land feels happy to see the wheat with its fruit, God will be pleased with us when we bear fruit. But what is this fruit-bearing life all about? Jesus calls the people who are compared to the wheat as the righteous ones. That is to have a righteous attitude, to say the right thing, to do the right thing, to live the right way even when it is difficult. Righteousness is an attitude we need to have. When we are faithful to God, we will be righteous too in His sight.

In our post-modern world we see a great emphasis on industrial expansion and further development of the already present resources. Unfortunately, some do not realize that all these developments and privileges remain as weed and unattainable for many who cannot afford them. It is not that progress is not necessary. But advances in technology and all sciences can be truly fruitful only when they include the poorest and the most vulnerable as its beneficiaries.

When we look around the world there are millions in need. It may look as though we really cannot make a difference. There is a very well-known story which says that a young man was very gently throwing star fish, which were on a seashore, into the ocean. Another person asks him: Why are you throwing starfish into the ocean? He replies: "The sun is up and the tide is going out. And if I don't throw them in, they'll die." Then the elder one said: "Don't you realize that there are miles and miles of beach with starfish all along it. You can't possibly make a difference." The young man listened politely. He then bent down, picked up another starfish, threw it into the ocean, and said, "It made a difference for that one."

The parable of the wheat and the weed encourages us in our support to the needy through the church and other charities. Together it is possible to make a difference in this world. And indeed, the greatest encouragement is that Christ is pleased with us when we are faithful in our calling.

The same parable ultimately teaches us that we have the potential to be faithful. Just as a farmer sows good seeds to have good produce, God has created us with the potential to be good, to be faithful. We are created to be faithful to God and to our fellow human beings.

Just as a good yield brings a smile to a farmer's face, faithful hearts bring a smile on the face of God. The real wheat which God is looking for is our faithfulness. The next parable will make this plain – that faithfulness requires offering ourselves to God.

It is not your success that God wants, but it is you

Many years back I used to preach at a church in India. That church was at the end of a street. There were houses on both sides and I used to walk along that street to get to the church on Sunday mornings. Most of the people who lived on that street came to the church. One Sunday while I was going to the church two people from two of the houses started arguing. I didn't know the reason until I spoke to them later. However, someone started ringing the bell at the church and I could hear one person saying to the other. The bell is ringing — I need to go to the church now. I will come back and see you. Those words made me think. Why do we go to church? Is it not to make peace with God? Is it not to make peace with God's people? Of course that is why we go to church.

Nevertheless, later I spoke to them and found out the reason for their argument. In rural Indian culture it is okay to ask why you were quarrelling or what the problem was – and it's not being nosy. However, back to the story. The reason was that one person owned two houses. He had given one house for rent. The person who rented the house had not paid the rent on time.

Jesus told another wonderful story. The owner of a vineyard had rented it out to some workers. In Palestine, this was a common practice. The equivalent in our society could be renting allotments or houses. But in Palestine those who rented vineyards paid either in cash or an agreed share of the wine. In this particular vineyard, the owner sent his servants to collect the rent. But those renting caught the servants and either beat them or killed them. They didn't want to pay the rent.

Here, Jesus is saying that God created the world and all of us. The world is God's vineyard. I, as the son of God, came to collect the "rent" which is your hearts and minds.

This parable makes it plain that this world is God's vineyard. He has given His vineyard, this world, to us for a short period of time to live and work in. We really need to pay the rent. The rent is not just paying some money although the Bible teaches that is part of Christian commitment.

The real rent that is due to God is a bit more than that. Our rent we owe to God is our hearts and our very life. Just as the owner of a vineyard expects his share of fruits from the vineyard, God expects that you and I will offer ourselves faithfully to Him Very often when we give, we are careful not to be affected. Those renting the vineyard too didn't want to be affected in any way. But it is when we are affected, maybe at least in a small way, by our faithfulness and faithful living – by our different way of living – God's blessings will be abundant. Of course, God doesn't want us to go get burnt out or exhausted but when our life and lifestyle changes, as we give God what is due to Him, He comes closer to us.

Remember, the most important message in the story is the trust of the owner. The owner trusts and gives the vineyard to the care of the tenants. God has trusted you and me and given this vineyard to us. You and I should show the same faithfulness God shows to us. God tells us – I trust you, you can do it, work for me in my vineyard.

To conclude this section, God owns the vineyard that is the world and everything in it. We are the rent that is due. Faithfulness is about committing ourselves into the hands of God. Committing ourselves into the hands of God is, no doubt, the real success of life. In the next sub-chapter, we will reflect on ways in which we can live humbly and simply before God. A God-inspired life surely includes overcoming pride and living differently.

Questions for discussion or reflection
1. What would a faithful life look like in our world today?
2. What can you do to cultivate a faithful heart?
3. Why do we sometimes struggle to be faithful to God?
4. What is righteousness? What is the difference between faithfulness and righteousness?
5. How can we commit all aspects of our life to God's glory? Is it possible at all?
6. God offered us His best in Jesus. What is the best you can offer to God?
7. We need God's help to live a faithful life. How can God help you to be faithful to Him?

4.3 Created not to be boastful but to be humble and simple before God

What does God require of you? To act justly, love mercy and walk humbly before the Lord.[10]

Pride makes us artificial and humility makes us real.–
(Thomas Merton)

St. Augustine, in his book Confessions, says that he wasn't humble enough to understand the Bible when he read it first time. Pride can blind us before God. As they say, "pride goes before a fall."

The biggest problem that keeps God away from fulfilling His purpose in our life is pride. When we tell God, I can do it, He leaves us on our own. Sooner or later, we realize that we fail in our own strength, and often painfully. We can also go astray doing what we want to do and not what God would like to see us do.

A story is told about a big rock by the side of a road. People who passed by admired the rock for its enormous size and strength. As the story goes, the rock began to feel proud of itself. One day a bird dropped a small seed on the rock. The seed began to germinate in the little dirt that was on the rock. Soon, a plant began to grow and its roots went deep. Within a few years the plant became a tree and the roots of the tree broke the rock into pieces. God often chooses the weak to shame the strong.

Before we move on, we need to be clear that humility is not weakness. It is not being a "doormat" to everyone. Instead, it is being strong and confident, so as to live not only for oneself but also for God and others. Humility can mean not claiming the rights, honor, prestige or even respect which people may feel are due to us but recognizing and acting on the belief that everyone (including us) is of equal worth and value and deserving of the same treatment.

Thankfully, the Bible is full of examples of people who humbled themselves before God. And God uses them to fulfill His purpose in them.

The Israelites were slaves under the Egyptians. The Egyptian Pharaoh began to oppress the Israelites as much as he could.

They used to make bricks for the Egyptians and they were given the required quantity of straw for that. But, in order to make more trouble for the Israelites, one day, the Pharaoh ordered that no straw should be given to the Israelites, but that they should still produce the same number of bricks as before. The Pharaoh had begun to think that there is no higher power above him.

In this context the interaction between God and Moses is worth mentioning. God called Moses and said, "I have chosen you to deliver my people from Egypt." What is very fascinating here is Moses' answer. He did not say that is absolutely fine. Neither did he say, "I have all the qualifications for that." But he humbled himself before God. He realized his weaknesses and unworthiness before God's holiness. In scripture, we read, "But Moses said to the Lord, O my Lord, I have never been eloquent, neither in the past not even now. I am slow of speech and slow of tongue." Then God replied, "Who gives speech to mortals? Is it not I, the Lord?" God strengthened him and said: "I will be with your mouth and teach you what you are to speak."[11] We know that later Moses led the Israelites out of Egypt.

It is when Moses humbled himself before God, God used him. It is a privilege and a joy to be used by God. Even today, when we humble ourselves before God, He strengthens us and does great things for us and through us.

Similarly, in the Book of Judges we read of Gideon. During Gideon's time the Israelites suffered in the hands of the Midianites. Whenever the Israelites planted seeds, the Midianites would come up against them. They would set up camp and destroy the produce of the land. The Israelites cried out to the Lord for help. In the Book of Judges we read that the angel of God appeared to Gideon and said, "Go in this might of yours and deliver Israel from the hand of Midian."[12] Gideon, too, humbled himself before God. He responded, "How can I deliver Israel? My clan is the weakest in Manasseh, and I am the least in my family." When Gideon said that he was among the least, God told him, I will be with you. Go in the strength which you have. God delivered the Israelites through Gideon.

Do we humble ourselves before God? God lifts us up when we humble ourselves before Him. God's light can be seen clearly when we puff out our own little candles.

It is not only in Old Testament times but also in New Testament times we read that God used people who humbled themselves before Him. In the Book of Acts, we see that Peter was a great leader of the church. Indeed, Jesus had told him that He would build His church on Peter. But, even Peter, who was physically strong, had humbled himself before Jesus during his calling. As we saw earlier, Peter and others in his boat had tried to catch fish throughout the night. Until morning they caught nothing. Jesus came to them and told them to put out into deep water and let down their nets for a catch. When they did so they caught plenty of fish. Realizing that Jesus was Lord, Peter fell down at Jesus' knees. Luke 5:8 says that Peter pleads to Jesus, "Go away from me, Lord, for I am a sinful man." That was a cry of utter humility and self-denial. He became the chief among the disciples.

Jesus chooses us not when we think that we are great but when we acknowledge that we are weak and inadequate.

John and James wanted a place on His right and His left when He will be in glory. But for Jesus, if we want to be great in God's kingdom, we need to learn to be the servant of all. He also said that the Son of Man came not to be served but to serve. When we kneel before God we can stand before the world with no fear.

Jesus humbled Himself and served others

As we have noted earlier, Jesus pointed out that the two most important things for which we are created are these. First, to love God and to serve Him and second, to love God's people and to serve them. They are the rocks we have to walk upon without drowning in the egos, selfishness, and celebrity culture, greed of various kinds and the evils and sins of the world.

Jesus not only taught people to serve God and to serve one another but also taught using examples from everyday life. Jesus told us a story of the Good Samaritan.[14] "Good Samaritan" today has become a catchy phrase to refer to people who do a good job. He also taught about visiting people in prison and feeding the hungry.[15] Further, He saw His role in this way: "I have come to proclaim good news to the poor, to bind the broken hearted and to set the captives free."[16]

Contrary to worldly greatness, Jesus measures greatness in terms of humble service, not status. Even the disciples argued about who deserved the most prominent position, but Jesus called Himself a servant and washed the feet of His disciples. Then He told them, "You call me Lord and Teacher and that is correct. Follow my example."

Interestingly, anyone can serve. It doesn't require a very specialized skill to be service-minded. For instance, anyone can stay back after a meeting to pick up rubbish or stack chairs. Or anyone can visit the lonely in a nursing home or their home in their spare time. Of course, you would need a DBS check but the point is first and foremost you need to be service-minded. What it requires is humility and right-mindedness more than anything else. And perhaps we also need to know that often we will go unnoticed when we serve humbly. But remember the Lord who washed the feet of His disciples watches you. You never go unnoticed in His sight.

This is well said by Henri Nouwen. In his words, "In order to be of service to others we have to die to them; that is, we have to give up measuring our meaning and value with the yardstick of others ... thus we become free to be compassionate."[17] When we base our worth and identity on our relationship with Christ, we are freed from the expectations of others, and that allows us to really serve them best.

Washing feet is the equivalent of being a shoeshine boy, a job devoid of status. But Jesus knew who He was. So, the task didn't threaten His self-image. He got up from the meal to wash the feet of His disciples. As we saw in Chapter 1, to live a God-inspired life we need to find our security in God.

As John Wesley superbly said, "Do all the good you can, by all the means you can, in all the ways you can, in all the places you can, at all the times you can, to all the people you can, as long as you can."[18]

The teaching and example of God in Christ should make us think and act. If more people have a humble and service-minded heart most of the problems related to injustice, hatred, greed and violence will be solved.

In fact, throughout His ministry Jesus, who washed the feet of His disciples, found His friends amongst the poor. The lives of the oppressed, the captives, the poor, the sick, these are the lives which became the center of Jesus' mission on earth. It is the lives of the have nots, the down and outs, those who live on the margins of society or have been abandoned by it altogether – human flotsam and jetsam – it is through interaction with these lives that God's purposes for our lives too can be uncovered.

It is humility and service that can bring us the greatest joy and contentment which nothing else can bring or match. The saints of God found joy and happiness in helping others, visiting the sick, listening to those in pain, taking the gospel to the most difficult places and bearing pain for others.

There are many who understood what Jesus meant by washing the feet of His disciples and then saying "follow my example." They understood that true joy and life are to be found in humble service for Christ's sake and His people's sake. All those who have accumulated millions do not find where true joy and life is. All those who have become celebrities do not find where true joy and life is. Even kings like Solomon who had thousands of wives said it was in vain. Then, who are the people who understand where true joy and life is? It is those who find joy and fulfillment in serving others humbly. Albert Schweitzer, a theologian famously said, "The only really happy people are those who have learned how to serve."

The disciples eventually understood that they needed to live by humbly serving others, following Jesus' example. They went throughout the world to serve God and His people.

As you read this, I would encourage you to emulate what Jesus did and wash the feet of others (whatever that might mean in your context metaphorically) so that you "demonstrate" your humility and make others emulate what Jesus did too. Thereby we can become collective witnesses to God.

Questions for discussion or reflection

1. Why do we sometimes struggle so hard to live a humble life?
2. Who are the biblical characters who inspire you to live a humble life?
3. Do you have a role model (e.g., a teacher) who inspired you to live differently?
4. How would you explain to someone that humility is not weakness?
5. Why do you think people are more attracted to the so-called celebrities than the real keyworkers in our society?
6. What are the ways we can demonstrate our humility in our world?
7. How would you differentiate between the character of an arrogant person and a humble person?

4.4 Run in such a way that you may win

All you need is the plan, the road map, and the courage to press on to your destination.
(Earl Nightingale)

To become 'unique,' the challenge is to fight the hardest battle which anyone can imagine until you reach your destination.
(A. P. J. Abdul Kalam)

We learned about humble and simple living overcoming pride in the last sub-chapter. In this section, we move on to explore ways in which we can win the race of life by the grace of God. St. Paul writes that life is like a running race. He says, " Run in such a way as to get the prize."[19] We are placed in this world by God to run the race of life as best as we can, with the help of God, just as athletes run to win. The good news is unlike a running race where only one will win, in the running race of life we all can win.

How do we do this? According to the New Testament, there are only two rules or principles to win the race of life. The first rule is to run by putting our complete faith and trust in God in Christ. And the second rule is to continue the good works that Jesus did.

The simple truth to bear in mind is that if an athlete wants to do well, both his/her legs need to be strong. Both legs need exercise and practice and both should be equipped and both should be sinewy. In running the race of life our two legs are faith and good works. Their importance cannot be overemphasized.

Faith as one leg to run the race

The disciples of Jesus ran the race of life with Him. They were able to do this because they put their faith in God in Christ. In the gospels, Jesus of Nazareth is often called a rabbi and His followers, disciples. A disciple was someone who had chosen to follow his rabbi as much as possible in order to learn everything he could from the rabbi and not just during formal teaching times.

In the Talmud there is a story about a disciple who hid under his rabbi's bed so that he would be present when the rabbi and his wife went to sleep. He was discovered, and the rabbi wanted to know what his best pupil was doing there. His response was this: "This too is Torah, and I need to learn." This commitment of the disciple to stay in the presence of the rabbi was stunningly expressed in the blessing: "May you always be covered by the dust of your rabbi." In other words, may you run with him so closely that the dust that his feet kicks up covers your clothing and face! Very much like a baby bear whose image of its mother is imprinted on its brain and puts its complete trust in its mother, disciples never want to let the rabbi out of their sight and they put their complete faith in him.

Today, faith is sometimes belittled and those who believe in God are frowned upon and considered old-fashioned by some. But the truth still remains. Only our faith in a power greater than us can sustain us when we fall down or decelerate in our running race. Only our faith will stand in good stead when it comes to progressing to the finish line. Only by faith we can know ourselves and our destination, which is God Himself. Here I remember a line from William Wordsworth's *Intimations of immortality*, "Trailing clouds of glory we come. From God, who is our home."[20] Clearly, God is our genesis too.

Thankfully, the Bible teaches that faith as small as a mustard seed is bound to grow. When you put your trust in God, your faith gives you the assurance that you will win the race of life.

Faith helps you start again when things go wrong and you fail. Faith is light in times of darkness. It is also faith that brings you the assurance of your sins being forgiven.

Faith has to be nurtured. In fact, we are asked to guard our faith because it is the treasure entrusted to us.[21] Worship and learning are the ways to protect and guard our faith.

If you are not a believer at the moment and if you are reading this you can always seek God. Seeking God is a lovely thing before the eyes of God. Keep seeking until God finds you. It is worth it because faith is essential in this race of life.

It is through faith we know that we are not alone in the

race of life. God is with us encouraging us, challenging us and strengthening us always.

If you have seen a mother hen look after her chicks, you will know that she can be fiercely protective of them snuggling together under her wings. Anyone who is perceived to harm little chicks is certain to be pecked by a mother hen. I still vividly remember how I was pecked several times by a mother hen despite having no intention to do any harm to the chicks. Even while a danger in the form of a fox lurks nearby, the helpless chicks crowd together under her warm body quite unaware of and unconcerned about any possible danger. No matter what the lurking danger is, they depend on their mother for protection. The fox as a predator is always there just as Satan is. They try to slip out now and then and her wing scoops them back up into the safety of her shelter. This is the picture of God that we all need to cherish – a protective, loving, warm, supportive, defending God – a mother hen who holds her chicks in a passionately sheltering sanctuary. Just as a mother hen never leaves her little ones alone, it is through faith that we will know that God never leaves us alone. Even when we fall, He picks us up and helps us start again.

However, faith is only one leg of an athlete who runs the race of life. Faith without good works is similar to limping in a race. So, we now look at the other leg we need to run without limping.

Good works as the other leg

A seven-year-old boy was freezing in the cold as he didn't have a jacket. An elderly woman saw him and took him to a shop and bought him a jacket, some more clothes and some sweets – indeed a gesture of kindness. The boy was very happy. He looked at her and asked her, "Are you God?" With a smile on her face she said, "No, I am one of God's children." The boy replied, "I thought you must be related." As this story points out there are always opportunities to do good works giving glory to God.

In a sense, service to humanity is worship of God.

Bonhoeffer, a theologian, famously said that Jesus was a man for others. It is true that Jesus, during His ministry, did little for Himself but plenty for others. He sided with the poor, encouraged the low in spirit, healed the sick and gave Himself to serve others.

Similarly, our faith needs to be put into action. In fact, the Book of James highlights the way in which believers need to live a balanced life. For James, faith and good works are like two sides of the same coin.

James challenges, "Do you think faith can save you?" To be precise, he is asking if faith without action is true faith? For him, faith should overflow with action. He goes on to say, "If a brother or sister is naked and lacks daily food and one of you says to them, go in peace, keep warm and eat your fill, and yet you do not supply their bodily needs, what is the good of that?"[22] So, for James, faith, if it has no works, is dead.

We need to find friends among the poor. When we do that, we are co-operating with Christ in his mission. The lives of the oppressed, the captives, the poor, the sick, these are the lives which become the center of Jesus' mission on earth. Jesus said, "And the King will reply, 'Truly I tell you, whatever you did for one of the least of these brothers of Mine, you did for Me.'"[23] This clearly establishes that when we do something to improve the living conditions of an impoverished person or persons, we really serve God. There can be no better example than Mother Teresa who came to be eulogized as the Saint of the Gutter for the good works that she did.

The good news is there are many models who have put their faith into action. To give you a few examples, in Britain alone in the last century there has been Bruce Kenrick, the first Chairman of Shelter, a charity organization whose work is inspiring and Chad Varah, a Vicar in London who founded the Samaritans which now receives 13,000 calls a day. Peter Benenson, the young lawyer who founded Amnesty International, which advocates compassion and lenience and acknowledges the influence of the compassion and humanity shown by Christ on him. Dame Cecily Saunders, the founder of the Hospice movement, declared that without the inspiration of Jesus' teaching and the strength given her by His Spirit, the problems she faced would have overwhelmed her. For these people, amongst many others faith and action go hand in hand. They cannot be separated.

However, sadly a modern day re-writing of the parable of the sheep and the goats may go something like this: "I was hungry and you formed a committee to investigate my hunger; I was homeless and you filed a report on my plight; I was sick and you held a seminar in London on the situation of the underprivileged and malnourished; I was in prison and you set up a Bible study group and a prayer group for reforming us; I was naked and you bought Café Direct and Traidcraft goods. You have investigated all aspects of my plight and yet I am still hungry, homeless, sick, naked and in prison."[24]

Precisely, the question we should all ask is what good works we are doing or can do. You can now appreciate that faith and good works are like two legs if we see life as a running race.

Be focused on the race of life knowing that the destination is one step closer every day

We can be focused on the race of life only by staying away from the junk and distractions of the world. Here are the common distractions we need to be cautious about. Love of popularity, power, material things and lust of the flesh can distract us from being focused on God and the good works He has called us to do.

Apart from the above temptations, people also get distracted by pain. We will devote the next chapter to looking at pain and suffering. Here, let us be mindful that we shouldn't give up on God. Turning our focus to God again and again is essential to keep ourselves on track or get back on track when we go astray.

Just as an athlete knows the importance of constant training, we need to train ourselves to be in constant communion with God.

Above all, it is by grace we win the race

Everything that the Father gives me will come to me, and anyone who comes to me I will never drive away; for I have come down from heaven, not to do my own will, but the will of him who sent me. And this is the will of him who sent me, that I should lose nothing of all that he has given me, but raise it up on the last day.[25]

How much goodness is good enough? How many good works are good enough?

Well, a God-inspired life is a life that relies on the grace of God. Of course, life is a test. But we cannot rely on our own strength to win. Everything we are we owe to God and everything we have is given to us by grace. It is through grace we are given the assurance of winning the race of life. There is nothing as wonderful as the grace of God. Having explored the significance of faith and good works, we will specifically explore ways in which we can overcome temptations with God's help and become a winner in His eyes.

Questions for discussion and reflection

1. Do you agree with Paul when he compares life to a running race? If yes/no, in what ways?
2. What do you think "following Jesus" in our everyday life means today?
3. What differences do you think faith in God makes in one's life?
4. How would you help someone who says that they would like to believe in God but are not able to?

5. Do you think both faith and good works are different sides of the same coin?

6. There is so much need in the world. How would you discern the "good works" God has called you to do?

7. Can you remember one or two instances in your life when you clearly received God's grace?

4.5 Ways to overcome temptations and trials

When tempted, no one should say, "God is tempting me." For God cannot be tempted by evil, nor does he tempt anyone; but each person is tempted when they are dragged away by their own evil desire and enticed.[26]

Do you really think it is weakness that yields to temptation? I tell you that there are terrible temptations which it requires strength, strength and courage to yield to. (Oscar Wilde)

It is obvious that this world has good and not so good things in it. In fact, there is a struggle constantly going on in all of us. There is a divine spark that inspires us to goodness, and there is an evil spark which tells us to walk in the worldly ways. For children who study, the divine spark would be saying that they need to devote themselves to creativity, recreation and their studies. They have to listen to their teachers, respect them and obey them. This will certainly enable them to come up in life. But the evil spark would be saying that they don't have to occupy themselves positively and let themselves be guided by their teachers. For those of us who are involved in various works, the divine spark would be saying that you need to be sincere in your work and you need to be friendly with your colleagues. The evil spark would be saying that you need not be bothered about others, you can have your own selfish ways. The divine spark also would be saying that we should not be discourteous but be altruistic towards our neighbors. As God in Jesus has shown His love for us, by example we too, should love our neighbors and be kind to them.

God wants us to keep the divine spark within our hearts as the driving force to do good things. This is explicable in terms of God's holiness and His hatred of evil. It is imperative that we know how we can tackle the trials and temptations we are faced with in life and emerge successfully. We do not have the strength in us to overcome all our temptations. We need God's help.

Learn the word of God

Jesus himself was tempted. He quoted the words of the scripture to triumph over his temptations and trials. A click of the mouse will bring on your computer screen verses that give you guidance and strength to resist temptations. For the benefit of those who don't use a computer or smart phone, here are three verses.

"Do not let your heart turn to her [a prostitute's] ways or stray into her paths. Many are the victims she has brought down; her slain are a mighty throng."[27]

"[T]he Lord knows how to rescue the godly from trials and to hold the unrighteous for punishment on the day of judgment."[28]

"On reaching the place, he said to them, 'Pray that you will not fall into temptation.'"[29]

Be alert, be on guard

Temptations come from everywhere. No one is immune to temptations in this world. The trials of life come unexpectedly too. It is wise to be alert so that we can identify temptations and trials and overcome them before it is too late.

Be in constant relationship with God

In times of temptations and trials, connect with God in prayer. I often wonder why even good people sometimes yield to the sin of corruption and the sins of the flesh. It is because often we try to overcome sins with our own strength. Our strength can fail us. We need God's power to help us. Only God can give us the wisdom, courage and strength to resist the temptations and deal with the trials of life. The best way to get God's help is to connect with God in prayer.

As we know, the branches connected to the vine produce good fruit. When we are connected with God in Jesus, we produce good fruits and become incapable of producing bad fruits. It is important for us to realize the import of the words of Jesus: "Without me you can do nothing."[30] It should follow from this that depending on God's grace and guidance is the best way to triumph over temptations. It should be a basic belief with us that we cannot do so with our own strength, but we can with God's strength. What could be stronger than God's strength? What could beat God's strength? Nothing! God's help is so enabling that it helps anyone who is connected with God to walk in the paths of righteousness in times of temptations and trials.

Seek not the World but God and His Kingdom first
Seeking God

Seeking God helps to overcome temptations. Recently, I met a parent who said, "I do not bring my children to Sunday school or church because they can decide whether they want to believe in God or not when they are grown-up." My response was if you don't bring them to church and if they don't listen to what's being taught and preached about God, as well as learn a little about why others believe, how can they make an informed decision? We need to seek God in all ways possible. In fact, we need to seek God until we find Him because it is His promise that those who seek Him will find Him. And God keeps His promises. When we seek God, our attention is on God and not on the temptations and trials the world throws at us.

From my own experience I can testify that those who seek God will find God sooner or later. A few years ago, I had to take the funeral service of a parishioner. I knew this parishioner quite well and I also knew that he did not believe in God. In the past he had told me that he had sought God long and hard, and yet he was not able to believe in Him. He added that one of my predecessors had helped him too. I listened to him carefully and just added "keep seeking." However, he sadly fell seriously ill and breathed his last. The family had asked me to take the funeral service at the crematorium. The authorized order of service repeatedly talks about faith. It also quotes biblical passages which say that those who believe in God in Christ will have eternal life. I went to the crematorium, and I was still struggling as to which words of comfort and hope I could give the family. I knew that the deceased didn't believe in God: he divulged it to me. As I was praying about it silently, I heard God speak clearly and loudly into my thoughts. I heard God say, *If I have accepted him what is your problem.* As you can expect, I felt a big relief and joy within myself. I loved this man and I was overjoyed to hear those words from God. I thanked God and took the service in peace. I had to conclude that day that God valued my parishioner seeking Him. As he had told me he had long and hard sought after God. What more could he do? He was in ICU for a few weeks before he died. Either he must have found God there or certainly he found God in His kingdom. Or to put it differently, God found him. Either way it doesn't matter. This experience taught me how much God loves us when we seek him. God reveals Himself to us sooner or later when we seek Him and persevere in seeking Him. There is no substitute for seeking God. Nowadays we can get some things only online. This involves effort. Similarly, the only possible way to get close to God is by spending time and energy to seek God. Seeking God is a joy. It is a reward in itself. It helps us keep our focus on the divine and not on temptations.

The prophet Jeremiah has this to say about seeking God:

When you search for me, you will find me; if you seek me with all your heart, I will let you find me, says the LORD, and I will restore your fortunes and gather you from all the nations and all the places where I have driven you, says the LORD, and I will bring you back to the place from which I sent you into exile.[31]

Obviously, Jeremiah writes this in a context of exile. Our life in this world is similar to a life in exile. We plan something and something else happens. We often wonder what's really happening. Nevertheless, even in this world of chaos and confusion we can seek God and find Him. It goes without saying that to live a God-inspired life we need to seek God.

James writes, "Draw near to God and he will draw near to you."[32] If we really wish to draw close to God, we need to make time for Him. These high moments in our life in which we seek God will make a tremendous difference to our life. It is a very wise idea to begin our days by seeking God diligently first. The psalmist sings:

"Happy are those who keep his decrees, who seek him with their whole heart, who also do no wrong, but walk in his ways."[33]

Seeking God constantly helps us to walk in His ways and receive the joy of God in our hearts every day. The joy of God in our hearts is our strength to face trials and tribulations and to overcome temptations.

Seeking God's Kingdom

To resist temptations and go through trials and tribulations with courage, it is vital that we need to derive strength from God and rely on His guidance. We need to focus on God's kingdom. When we do so our life changes for the better.

Historically speaking, we read of different kings ruling different kingdoms. There was the kingdom of Alexander the Great, there was the kingdom of King James and so on. Those kingdoms had geographical boundaries in a historical period of time. The Kingdom of God is similar to that but is not exactly the same. It is similar in the sense that both kingdoms ruled by earthly kings and by God have only one ruler. Different kings ruled different kingdoms and God rules His Kingdom. But a kingdom ruled by an earthly king and the Kingdom ruled by God are different in the sense that when the earthly kings rule you don't have a choice. If you live within the geographical boundary of a kingdom ruled by an earthly king you have to obey the king's rules and abide by his law, otherwise you could be exiled or executed. But, unlike earthly kings, God gives us the freedom to obey His laws and abide with Him or reject His rule and live as we like.

To put it differently, it is not geographical boundary that determines whether we live in God's Kingdom or not. It is decided in our hearts. If our hearts are filled with God's Holy Spirit and His glory, we are part of his Kingdom – if not we live outside His Kingdom. God desires that we accept Him, put Him first in our lives and abide in His Kingdom.

I know it is very easy to write this, but difficult to put into practice. The truth really is that we yield to temptations and struggle while grappling with trials and tribulations when we do not let God rule our lives. Often, we do not seek His rule in our lives, marriages, home, family and lifestyle. We want to keep control of our own lives rather than give them to God so that he can bless our lives and make them holy. While we live in this world we seek many things – some important and some not so important. Jesus says that when you seek God's Kingdom all that you need will be provided.

To seek God's Kingdom is to put God at the center of our lives. Some of you must have heard about Sadhu Sundar Singh. He was a saint who lived in India. His mother was not a Christian but a Sikh. She lived and died a Sikh. But the saint was a convert. He was born into a Sikh family then he became a Christian. One day, Sundar Singh's friends told him, "We very well know your faith, your pious life and the good things you do and we also know you will go to heaven. But please tell us if your mother will be in heaven or not." Sadhu Sundar Singh replied, "I do not know whether I, or my mother, will be in heaven or not. But I know that a place without my mother cannot be heaven for me."

Similarly, a place without God cannot be the Kingdom of God to us. Scripture tells us God loves us just as a mother loves her child. If we know that God is with us and He is part of our lives, we are already in God's Kingdom. I wonder what your answer would be if someone were to ask if you are in the Kingdom of God or not? Am I in God's Kingdom? Is God with me and am I with God?

To seek His Kingdom is to remove any hurdle that prevents our relationship with God. Seeking God's Kingdom rather than a worldly kingdom will change our outlook on life and thereby help us resist temptations and face trials and tribulations.

Seeking God's Righteousness

Before the time of Moses, in the Old Testament, we read that it was right to punish someone seven times for a misdemeanour. So, if a person beats another once he or she could be beaten seven times in return. Then Moses teaches that that is not right. If a person broke the law once you could only punish that person once in return. It was considered that to be righteous was to do like for like only once. But later Jesus came along and said, "Moses said that because of your hard-heartedness. There is no need to do that even once. Instead – love your enemies. Bless those who curse you and pray for those who hurt you." We see a progression in Jesus' understanding of righteousness.

Our love for God and His people including our enemies and not material riches or other transient pleasurers of the world, is what will help us get our priorities right and resist temptations and tribulations with wisdom and courage.

To conclude, overcoming temptations is our goal. However, we need not live without the assurance of past sins and guilt. At worship services in church, we have the opportunity to repent, confess our sins and guilt and receive God's forgiveness. When God forgives all is forgiven indeed. We can also bring ourselves before God in prayer each day so that He can cleanse us and start afresh again.

Questions for reflection or discussion

1. How can we keep the divine spark within our hearts alive in our everyday life?
2. How would you help a friend overcome a temptation if he/she opens up to you?
3. Do you believe that you need God's help to overcome the many temptations in life? If yes, why?
4. What are the different tools God has given us to overcome temptations?
5. Do you take time to seek God every day? If yes, do you find it easy?
6. What do you think God's kingdom is? What are ways we can seek God's kingdom?
7. Can one's love for God and others play a vital part in overcoming the trials and tests of life? If yes, how can we grow in our love for God and His people?

Chapter 5

Life Is a Struggle—
God-Inspired Life Is to Know That God
Stays with Us and Will Get Us Through

5.1 Hold onto God in times of suffering and pain

We are afflicted in every way, but not crushed; perplexed, but not driven to despair; persecuted, but not forsaken; struck down, but not destroyed....[1]

When the world pushes you to your knees you're in the perfect position to pray.
(Rumi)[2]

In the previous chapter we learned that we can receive God's forgiveness in and through repentance and prayer. We also explored ways in which we can overcome any temptations. In this chapter, we will explore the problem of pain and suffering. We will learn ways in which we can cope with the struggles of life which is an important dimension that we cannot ignore.

Life is a struggle. The truth is either we are in the middle of a painful problem or getting out of one or heading towards one. At one point or another, everyone learns that life is a struggle. Some people look at life as having ups and downs. There are times when everything is fine and perfect. We are as happy as we can be. But there are also times when we are in distress, pain and tears. We can lose hope; everything around us can look dark and unbearable.

There are other people who don't think that life is about ups and downs. They think that life is like a railway track. Just as there are two tracks on the rail path, for them, life always

143

has two tracks. There are always good things which make us happy and at the same time there are bad things which make us struggle. Nevertheless, no matter how we look at life, pain and suffering are real.

Spiritual thinkers often say that there are two types of suffering. One is moral suffering and the other one is natural suffering. Moral sufferings are the ones that are caused by humans. For example, someone drinks and drives and kills an innocent child, or someone murders an innocent person. Human struggle for power, position and money constitutes a moral problem. Moral suffering can be very painful but it can be avoided to a large extent if we work towards it. However, there are also the natural calamities. A few examples are the recent coronavirus pandemic, earthquakes, landslides, lightning attacks and illnesses beyond our control.

Nonetheless, despite the cause, we do struggle in life. We struggle because of our own mistakes. We struggle because of others' mistakes and we also struggle when it is neither our fault nor anyone else's fault but when the nature of life mercilessly hits us. We struggle when we face failures in life and we struggle when we or our beloved ones are sick or ill. We all struggle when we face physical, emotional, mental, financial or relational problems in life. We struggle when we are bullied or belittled by others. We struggle when we lose a loved one. We can ask why me? Why suffering?

Biblically, the answer to the question of suffering is actually simple. It is because we live in a fallen and broken world. This world is not how God intended it to be. He gave us freewill but unfortunately humanity chose to misuse the freewill and sin entered the world and corrupted it. To put it in terms of physics, the cause is disobedience and the effect is suffering.

Some people tend to think that God causes pain and suffering. This is not true. God is good. St. Anselm said that the greatest good is God. Spiritual thinkers also claim that God is the source of goodness. God doesn't cause pain and struggle. However, the Bible undeniably says that God allows suffering. And suffering is real. Accordingly, Christianity and other major religions don't shy away from the reality of suffering. But God uses our pain constructively. We devote this sub-chapter to look at this.

1, To build our life

It is a fact that the struggles in our life can bring strength to us. Paul writes, "No temptation has overtaken you that is not common to man. God is faithful, and he will not let you be tempted beyond your ability, but with the temptation he will also provide the way of escape, that you may be able to endure it."[3] Without struggles we wouldn't know what the opposite is which is joy, contentment and life in its fullness. Without struggles we wouldn't grow strong either. We know that birds can push their little ones to get out of their comfortable nests and fly. It might look like a cruel thing to do. Even so, the mother bird knows that in the long term the struggle of learning to fly will be good for its little ones. God wants the best for us. He might allow struggles and pains in our life to make us stronger and better. Often when we look back at our life, we learn this but when we are going through our struggles it is hard.

In the Old Testament, very often when people go astray from God they end up in exile or in another calamity. In distress and slavery, they often look unto God. And God delivers them and heals them of their shame. Here, God is allowing a life of slavery and struggle to teach His people to stay close to Him. God allows suffering when people treat each other unjustly too. Prophets like Amos and Hosea again and again warn people to live a righteous and just life. When they fail, God allows struggle not because God hates them but He hates injustice, evilness, selfishness and arrogance.

In the New Testament, Peter reaffirms that struggles can make us a stronger person. They can help us grow and improve our behavior. In his words,

> *even if now for a little while you have had to suffer various trials, so*
> *that the genuineness of your faith – being more precious than gold*
> *that, though perishable, is tested by fire – may be found to result in*
> *praise and glory and honour when Jesus Christ is revealed.*[4]

So, when we go through struggles it is wise to ask why God has allowed them but not dwell there. We move on to ask where does He want to take us through this? Is God telling us something that we need to listen to?

Hundreds of doctors, nurses, psychologists, social workers and philosophers testify to the fact that the struggles they had faced in the past had made them better people. Many say they chose their career to serve others who struggle. Everyone faces struggles in life. Often, God brings healing in one way or another.

It might be that God has allowed a struggle in your life and got you out of it too to inspire you to serve others in a special way in the future. However, when we are in the middle of long-term pain and struggle, this approach wouldn't be of much help. It is entirely possible that even out of this long-term suffering and pain, some good might emerge. The next sub-chapter will deal with what we can do in those situations. Nevertheless, it is a fact that God allows suffering to make us strong, confident, and to rely upon His goodness.

2, To test our faith

The Book of Job talks about extreme and prolonged suffering in the life of Job. Job was a righteous man and that appears to be a problem too. Satan seems to have become jealous of Job's righteous and holy life. Satan gets God's prior permission to test him. Notably it is not God who tests him, but Satan. Job loses all his material possessions as well as his children. He is afflicted with wounds and unbearable physical pain. His wife tells him to curse God and die.[5]

However, he doesn't give up. He lets God be God in his life even in the midst of huge losses, constant physical pain and mental anguish. He did not lose faith in God. Job knew that God would have a plan. The Book of Job has been of massive comfort, support and strength to many people of God in times of pain and struggle of all kinds. In fact, the Book of Job holds out a great message of hope for us – the entire humankind.

Traditionally it has been thought that our sin is the root cause of pain and suffering. The Book of Job teaches us that the most righteous people can struggle too. Even the innocent and the pious ones are not immune to pain and suffering. So, why be righteous? Why be pious? Why try to live a just and holy life? Because the righteous know God's strength, peace and light, even in the midst of the darkest times in life and the most difficult days of life. They also have the hope that things will get better with God's help which is the greatest hope and privilege anyone could have in this life.

It is unfortunate that many, particularly in the West, find it hard to believe in God because life is a struggle. Of course, you only have to read newspapers or visit hospitals to see the extent of human suffering. There is an incomprehensible amount of pain and unspeakable sum of tragedies in this world. Often what one human being can do to another person to damage his/her life is unconceivable. And there are pains and sorrows beyond our control too. We all experience this. However, Job believed in God. He chose to trust God. He knew God personally. God delighted in Job when he trusted God even in the deepest valleys of suffering. The end of the story is good news. The Book of Job is a classic case of a "tragedy" becoming a "divine comedy." Job is blessed beyond his understanding. God will delight in us too when we lean on God and put our trust in Him as Job did – even in times of great trouble and misfortune. Remember, God has all eternity to shower blessings on us.

Interestingly, I have come across people who find faith for the first time in the midst of deep pain. One of my friends who didn't believe in God testified that at the funeral service of his child he found the peace and warmth of God for the first time. Mindboggling, but that was his experience.

The Bible says God is close to the broken-hearted. He never forsakes us. He is there caring for us even when we feel forlorn. Trusting God's presence with us even when we don't feel like it will help us get through the unfathomable tests in life.

3, To reveal God's glory

One day the disciples of Jesus asked Him about a man who was born blind. It was in a context where any and every struggle in life was seen as an effect of sinful life. In that situation they enquired of Jesus about the man born blind. They asked if it was his sin that he was born blind or whether it was his parents' sin. Jesus answered, "Neither this man nor his parents sinned; he was born blind so that God's works might be revealed in him."[6] Jesus then spat on the ground, made mud, put it on the blind man's eyes and asked him to go and wash in the pool of Siloam, which means "sent." He went and washed and he saw with his own eyes for the first time.

Often, we don't know why a period of suffering comes into our life. We could ask what sin have we committed. God heals many millions of people through doctors, nurses, counselors, or prayers. Sometimes the healing comes through a combination of many of these service-minded people. When we are delivered from the suffering, we realize that we struggled so that the glory of God could be revealed.

Going through difficult times in life is what teaches us who we really are. It is during those times we know who our real friends are too. God's healing of our struggles is the most powerful way we learn what God can do, and thereby enables us to see a glimpse of God's glory revealed in our lives too. When

God helps us get through one struggle, we gain the trust that He will be with us throughout our lives.

4, To draw us close to him

In spite of the reason for our struggle it is wise to get hold of God in our prayer. Our purpose of life is to learn to trust God even on the most difficult days of our life. No one says that it is easy. Failures, betrayals, losses, shocking diagnoses, are quite common. But hold on to God and know that God has a plan and purpose for you. When one door closes God opens a better door for His people. The crucial thing to do is to continue to trust in God and hold on to Him.

Questions for reflection or discussion

1. Can you remember one person who helped you in a time of struggle? What was the most helpful thing they said or did?
2. Can you think of any difficulty that you faced in the past that has made you a stronger and a wiser person?
3. Some say that they have lost their faith seeing the sufferings in the world. What would you tell them?
4. In what ways do you think faith in God brings comfort and hope in times of suffering and pain?
5. Do you think God allows sufferings in our lives for His purposes? If yes, what do you think His purposes might be?

5.2 God-inspired life is to know grace, love, peace and hope amidst struggle

In the previous sub-chapter, we learned that God invites us to hold on to Him in difficult times. In this section, we move on to explore ways in which God helps us when we face struggles in life.

"Yes, life is a struggle, but His grace is sufficient for thee."

This is the reply which Paul was given by Jesus when he struggled and prayed for healing. The good news is that God tells us that God's grace will carry us through even in this life with failures and sufferings. But what is grace? How does it work?

My grace is sufficient for thee

Everything that is good is grace. Grace simply is receiving the gifts from God we do not deserve. Our life itself is grace. The fact that we exist is grace. Our every breath is grace. All the good things we do with our life are the result of God's grace. In times of struggle grace is to have the assurance that God knows our pain and our weakness; His strength and comfort will carry us through. Above all, the presence of God with us every moment is grace.

St. Paul had an illness. There have been many speculations as to what was the problem which Paul might have had. They range from impairment in his eyes to hurting piles. We, in fact, don't know exactly what the problem was. He called it a thorn in his flesh. Whatever it might have been, God still used him to do great things for Him. His all-sufficient grace was more than enough for Paul at least in four kinds of struggles he faced:

1, Grace was sufficient for Paul to carry on with his work with the "thorn in his flesh." It helped him move on – to have a new normal life. Thanks to God's grace the "thorn in his flesh" could not hamper his trust in God in Christ.

2, Grace was enough for Paul despite his own illness to write about God's comfort to those in distress. Paul comforted and uplifted the churches of his time through his epistles. It became possible due to the all-sufficient grace. In II Corinthians 1. 3–7, he even writes brilliantly about joy. In his letter to the Philippians the word "joy" occurs 16 times – a clear indication that he was joyous despite all the sufferings in his life. For Paul, it is God's grace in the midst of suffering that lends greater meaning to life, fortifies life and enables us to live as true witnesses to God.

3, Paul faced so much opposition in many different ways in his participation in God's ministry. He was stoned, beaten and imprisoned amongst other painful tragedies that happened to him both on land and in the sea. Grace helped him not to give in. It is the glory of God that it is in our weakness where we see the wonder of grace more clearly.

4, Paul was mocked and belittled. He says, "When I am weak, I am strong." In another instance he says, "I will boast only about the cross." That is the grace of grace. All his life Paul was up against challenges and in all his life he never gave in. That was the work of the all-sufficient grace. Grace inspired Paul to face slander and mockery with grace.

John Newton, who sold slaves but later became a devout priest for God in Christ, writes about the amazing grace which opened his eyes. Similarly, Philip Yancey writes a book about what is so amazing about grace.[7] For him, grace is receiving the amazing forgiveness from God when we ask for it even though we don't warrant it. People of God knew that it's not just in the great things of life but also in the small things in life that the grace of God is present.

The point here is that people of God in the past knew that if God allows suffering and pain in their lives, He will also help them to get through it. Paul himself says, "God is faithful, and he will not let you be tested beyond your strength, but with the testing he will also provide the way out so that you may be able to endure it."[8] Even when there is no healing in the exact way we would like to, He promises to stay with us. God keeps His promises. His ways are always higher than ours.

The proposition is that we should know that even when we are in the midst of a problem or a struggle, God's grace is available. Even as we are inclined to seek help from professional experts we must remember to pray for healing and grace. Grace heals. God is full of grace so that you are fully justified to believe and hope that the best is yet to come.

Know the closeness of God's Love

Yes, we do struggle, but His love is sufficient for thee.

People of God who went through excruciating suffering testify that they often knew God's love even in the midst of pain and suffering. In difficult times when God seemed absent and even when they couldn't feel God's presence, they knew that God was with them. Why? It is because those people of God knew the nature of God. God promises never to forsake us or leave us alone. Isaiah writes,

> Shout for joy, you heavens; rejoice, you earth; burst into song, you mountains! For the LORD comforts his people and will have compassion on his afflicted ones. But Zion said, "The LORD has forsaken me, the Lord has forgotten me. Can a mother forget the baby at her breast and have no compassion on the child she has borne? Though she may forget, I will not forget you! See, I have engraved you on the palms of my hands; your walls are ever before me."[9]

It is comforting to note that God doesn't find anything else more precious to inscribe on his hands other than you and me. God is faithful and He promises to stay with us in our deepest valley of suffering. As Psalm 23 says, "Even though I walk through the valley of death, I fear no evil for you are with me." David went through personal difficulties and faced many attacks from his enemies. Psalm 23 tells us that what kept its author, King David, going, was the assurance of knowing God's closeness to him.

However, you might ask what about the words of the psalmist in psalm 22 "My God, my God why have you forsaken me?" Does God forsake us? Jesus repeated these words on the cross. So, is it true that God forsakes us?

There is a popular poem about a person who looked back at his life in his twilight years. In that poem, life is seen as a journey of walking on a seashore. Most of the time the footprints of two people are found on the sand. He readily understands that they are God's and his own. However, in some places there are only one person's footprints. The man realizes that these footprints have occurred in times of pain and struggle in his life. He feels that God may have left him alone during his difficult days. He complains to God. And God replies that the one person's footprints that he has found are not his, as he has thought, but God's. Everything unravels when God adds, "I carried you during times of pain and suffering." The poem ends with these evocative words,

> The Lord replied, "My son, My precious child,
> I love you and would never leave you.
> During your times of trial and suffering,
> when you see only one set of footprints,
> it was then that I carried you."[10]

In the New Testament Jesus promises that you and I are never alone. Jesus says, *Remember I am with you always, to the end of the age.*[11]

In the gospels we read that Jesus left the scene when his opponents tried to seize him. For instance, in John 10. 39 we see that while the Jews who didn't believe Jesus tried to catch Him, He escaped from them. However, when His disciples were in times of need, He didn't leave them alone. To point out one example, he didn't leave the disciples embarrassed at their inability to heal a boy who had seizures.[12] He took it upon Himself to heal the boy. Further, he didn't disappear from the boat which was caught in a storm with the disciples on board. He quelled their fears. No one who came to Jesus with their struggles for help went away disappointed. That is incredible, yet amazingly true. That is love of God in Jesus for His people.

In times of struggle, God invites us to look unto Him in prayer. He wants us to know His love for us. God is at work even when it doesn't feel like it. If today is Good Friday for you, be assured that Easter is coming. Perhaps Shelley derived his inspiration for the line, "If Winter comes, can Spring be far behind?"[13] from resurrection following crucifixion.

Know the peace which this world cannot give

Yes, we do struggle but His peace is sufficient for thee

Jesus says, *Peace I leave with you; my peace I give to you. I do not give to you as the world gives. Do not let your hearts be troubled, and do not let them be afraid.*[14]

Paul writes, *And the peace of God, which surpasses all understanding, will guard your hearts and your minds in Christ Jesus.*[15]

Peace is a gift from God. Even in the midst of deep pain God invites us to feel his presence and peace. It might seem almost impossible but seeking God in the midst of pain is the best thing we can do. Where else would you find the peace you need? What do you do when doctors say that they can't do anything more? What do you do when your loved one is on their deathbed or taken away from you? What do you do when you face a big failure in life?

God is there even in the midst of our struggles and pain. Psalm 34. 18 says, *The LORD is near to the broken hearted, and saves the crushed in spirit.*[16] C. S. Lewis famously said, "God whispers to us in our pleasures, speaks in our conscience, but shouts in our pains: it is His megaphone to rouse a deaf world."[17]

There are numerous verses in the Bible that invite us to bring our concerns and burdens to God in prayer. Amongst others, Peter writes, "Cast all your anxiety on him, because he cares for you."[18] Jesus himself invites us to cast our burdens unto him.[19] When we cast our burdens to Jesus, we need to believe that God has heard our prayers and knows what is best for us. Waiting for God patiently is often essential. In the midst of all struggles, seek for God's peace in prayer.

I have found God's presence in the most painful days of my life. The problem was still there but knowing God's peace meant it would be alright. A few years ago, I was with my dad in hospital. He had high PSA which meant prostate cancer. Everything looked gloomy for me. Not knowing what to do I sat there and prayed to God. I found God's peace and light in that difficult situation. God never promised a pain-free life. His promise is to be with us during the ups and downs of life every day.

Of course, I have to concede here that seeking professional support in appropriate situations is fine. At the same time, I wish to make my point that seeking the peace of God during pain and suffering brings great solace. Healing and consoling need not be separated from each other. They can co-exist. It is God who blesses us with the knowledge and methods to alleviate pain as much as possible.

In England, God provides us help through the NHS and other professionals. It is important that we seek medical and other appropriate help. Of course, prayer is no substitute for medical help. Still, it cannot be denied that patients who have faith in God immensely benefited from prayer. In fact, both – medical help and prayer – should go hand in hand. God often chooses to heal and make us whole through the agency of doctors, nurses, therapists, and learned professionals. It would be foolish not to make use of the gifts God has placed in them.

While I was struggling with ill health, people from the local parish church visited me as much as they could. One of them took me to the doctors several times. I found God's peace in their kind words and acts of goodwill. God can bring peace to someone in pain through you and me. It is a major part of our calling that we say words of comfort and peace to the ones who struggle in life. Also, when you go through struggles, get all help possible.

Christian hope is not just optimism but blessed assurance

Yes, we do struggle but His hope is sufficient for thee.

The hope that God gives us is not mere optimism or positivity but it is blessed assurance.

We are not promised a painless, struggle-free life. But there is always hope before us. As Julian of Norwich puts it succinctly, "All will be well." There are no "ifs" and "buts." There are no "maybes" or "perhaps." God always delivers His people at the right time and in His marvelous ways. He works beyond our expectations and imagination both in natural and supernatural ways to bring us healing and hope. We will move on to illustrate the significance of waiting for God when we face pain and suffering in the next sub-chapter.

Questions for discussion and reflection

1. Grace is not a word people use very often in their conversations. Why do you think this is the case?
2. Is it true that we better understand the need for grace on a bad day than when everything works normally in our lives?
3. Have you experienced God's love even in a difficult situation?
4. What could the words of Jesus, "Cast your burdens unto me" in an emotional as well as practical sense mean?
5. What could you do to channel God's peace in a difficult situation?
6. Is there a difference between worldly hope and Christian hope?

5.3 Waiting for God amidst suffering and pain

[T]hose who wait for the LORD *shall renew their strength, they shall mount up with wings like eagles, they shall run and not be weary,*

they shall walk and not faint.[20]

Being patient is a virtue. For Paul, it is a fruit of the spirit.[21] In our world of instant culture no one wants to wait. For example, some are not happy to wait until they have saved enough money to buy a product, but they buy with credit cards which costs them more money as they have to pay the interest too. One unwitting consequence is that some sadly become debt-ridden.

However, the scripture says that sometimes waiting is the appropriate and wise thing to do. But the question is whether it is possible to wait for God at all. The Psalmist says, "If I go up to the heavens, you are there; if I make my bed in the depths you are there."[22] How do we wait for God who is present everywhere?

Waiting for God is not something passive; it is active. Waiting for God is not like waiting for a train. It is to be more active than that. To wait for the Lord is to make a conscious attempt to see the invisible; waiting is endeavoring to hear the tender voice of God; it is opening our hearts and our whole being to feel his presence with us. It requires us to keep our mind, body and spirit active. Like those who study painting see better at an art exhibition, when our spiritual eyes and ears are well developed and trained, we more readily find God.

Prophet Isaiah says that it is important that we wait for God. How profound and worth heeding this advice of Isaiah is to the Israelites. This is clear in its context. Isaiah chapters 40 and 41 were written in a situation of great suffering and pain. It was written around 547 BCE when the Israelites were in exile in Babylon. Obviously, living as slaves in a foreign country is not easy. The Israelites were humiliated and demoralized by the Babylonians. Psalm 137 talks about the condition of the Israelites in Babylon. Verse one says, "By the rivers of Babylon, as we sat down, we wept when we remembered Zion." As the days passed by, life became more painful. It was in this circumstance that Isaiah said to his audience who were weary, faint and trembling,

"Wait for the Lord, for those who wait for the Lord will fly like eagles, they will run and walk." Isaiah brings comfort and hope by saying that doors will open for those who wait for the Lord.

Isaiah here focuses more on what needs to be done to mediate pain and suffering than on analyzing the cause of it. This needs special mention because the Israelites generally believed that sin caused suffering. Isaiah is more pragmatic than dogmatic. He speaks as if God had permitted Israelites to be in exile, so that they were in a position to turn to God more faithfully and wait for him. This, however, did not mean that they should intentionally take suffering upon them. The point is that, for Isaiah, the days of Israelites in Babylon were a period of pain and suffering. It was a means through which the Israelites would understand the glory of God once again. It is akin to Jesus saying about the blind man who was healed, "This happened so the power of God could be seen in him."[23]

Waiting for God requires complete trust in God

These words of Isaiah are words of comfort and encouragement even to us in situations of pain and hopelessness but waiting for God is only possible if we can trust Him fully. Although we may outwardly look free, we are not free from suffering and anxiety. Regarding our own situation, we suffer while we or our dear ones are ill, we suffer when we face failures, we suffer due to moral guilt and sometimes we suffer due to others' mistakes. For Isaiah, in any situation, people who wait for the Lord will not be ashamed. Isaiah 49:23 says, "They shall not be ashamed that wait for God." We are invited to trust this.

Simone Weil, a French philosopher has a book titled *Waiting for God*. She writes, from her experience, "Affliction makes God appear to be absent for a time. A kind of horror submerges the whole soul. During this absence there is nothing to love. The soul has to go on loving in the emptiness, or at least to go on wanting to love, though it may only be with a minute part of itself. Then, one day, God will come to show himself to this soul and reveal the beauty of the world to it, as in the case of Job."[24] It is true that throughout history, for people who waited for the Lord, He has remained the rock of peace, the unfailing comforter and the trustworthy companion. Sometimes we want to know God very quickly. But, often the more we are able to wait for God the greater the reward is. The more we love God the more we can wait for Him. The more we wait the more reliable we become for God.

A king wanted to reward the best person of his kingdom. Many tests were conducted and finally three were selected. Those three began to do equally well in all further tests. At last the king decided to have a running race. On the day before the race, the king sent his minister to all three of them, separately, to say – before you start running – wait for a secret signal from the king.

On the next day, when the start whistle was given, one began to run. Tempted by that the second one also ran. They reached the finish line at the same time. The third one was very attentively looking at the king for the signal. Then the king said to him, "I know that you would have run equally well. But I did not know that you would wait for me." The king rewarded him

Although waiting for God may be something that requires our complete attention, at times, we may not find it easy to wait. But, the ability to wait comes from understanding who God is. Waiting for God requires the realization and acceptance of God's omnipotence and human frailty. It requires acknowledging our dependence on God. It requires our willingness to wait. Above all, waiting for the Lord requires our absolute faith in God. It requires the ability to believe that God is reliable, God will not fail and God knows better. Waiting for God is exercising confidence in God's timing and help during difficult times. It requires offering a refreshing way out of ourselves.

Waiting for God needs to be a regular practice

Waiting for the Lord is something we should practice regularly rather than seeking His help only during difficult situations. Paul had specific times when he waited to hear from Christ. It is when we give time to God in Christ that He directs and guides our life. Our time with God alone can help us check if we are on the right track. The church father John Chrysostom famously said, "He who waits for Jesus' coming will perform works worthy of His joy." He is also wise to say that we need to wait for Christ's coming to us now in a particular sense and not just in the general sense of his coming at the end. Christ's coming is not to be viewed as an event that is to happen at a distant point in time in some unforeseeable future but as an ongoing and perennial event involving communion with God. The more you accept Christ the more God comes to you. Of course, it is certain that Christ's second coming is sure to happen eventually in its literary sense but when God alone knows. We do wait for trains and planes. It is an everyday experience that we wait for the traffic lights. Nevertheless, do we have the practice of waiting for God? Do we spend at least some time listening to God every day? Waiting for God is a gateway to understanding. In fact, God's grace and our effort are necessary for successful living. Where God's grace and human effort coincide, victory and happiness are sure to prevail.

Paul writes that "Christ will reward him and not only him, but all those who wait, with love, for Christ to appear."[25] This can also mean that, according to Paul, it is not just during times of suffering and pain but our entire life which is meant for waiting for Christ. Paul used his erudition as well as his skills for his ministry. He preached to various churches and his writings find a remarkable place in the New Testament. What is important for us to note is that, for Paul, all that he does is an expression of his waiting for Christ. For him, waiting for Christ is a process in which one witnesses Christ in all that one does. Knowing from experience that waiting for Christ is the most joyful experience, and it has the worthiest reward, Paul encourages Timothy to wait for Christ in and through all that he does and receive the same reward.

We are involved in various kinds of works and we have many responsibilities at home, at church and in the wider society. Some people say that they wait for Christ when they pray. But how do they wait for Christ when they get into their daily routine and work. Paul's words help us here. When we have the practice of waiting for Christ, He begins to abide with us. We begin to have the assurance and confidence that Christ is with us in all that we do. All good things that we do, whether we realize it or not, will be an expression of our waiting for Christ. It is in this sense, Paul writes to the Ephesians, no matter if we are called to be apostles, or prophets or teachers[26] (and here we may add the different works we are involved in), what matters is that our entire life should manifest that we wait for God.

Waiting for God is trusting God's timing

There is a story of an elderly mother who had three sons. The sons had left their home and they led their own lives. One Easter, they decided to send gifts to their mother. The eldest son bought a big house or a mansion and sent the documents to his mother. The second one bought a luxurious car and sent it with a driver to his mother. The third son knew that his mother was deeply religious. She used to read the Bible and now her eye-sight was not good enough to read it. So, he bought a parrot and trained it for months to say different biblical verses and he sent it to her. After a while, the mother wrote thank you letters to them. To the first one she wrote, "Thank you for the mansion but I can't maintain it, all that I need is the one room in which I live now. Anyhow, thank you for your kindness." To the second one she wrote, "Thank you for the car but I do my shopping at the shops nearby and I don't have the health to travel. Anyhow, thank you for your kindness." She hadn't even realized that the third son's gift was a parrot. So, she wrote to the third son. "Thank you very much for your gift. I liked it so much. The little chicken was very delicious."

Often, the gifts we give are unexplained and inappropriate. But the gifts of God are explained through the scripture, they are appropriate and timely. The greatest of God's gifts to His people is God Himself. God gives himself as a comfort to His people.

People who wait for God in prayer are sure to receive His comfort at the right time. God's timing is always better than our timing. God brings comfort to His people directly. However, God can also use others to bring comfort to you. For example, God says to the prophet Isaiah "Comfort, O Comfort my people."[27] Notably, for Isaiah, it is not some God who comforts some people but it is their own God who comforts His own people.

God is the possession of people who wait for Him. It is true that God has given himself as a gift of comfort to His people from the beginning – throughout centuries – up until today. Just like it is a comfort to have a friendly neighbor to whom we could turn to at any time – it is a comfort to know that God is with us and we could confidently wait for Him.

God in Jesus is already waiting for you

In Revelation 3:20, the story is turned upside down. When Isaiah and Paul say that we need to wait for the Lord, Jesus says, "Behold, I stand at the door and knock. If anyone hears my voice and opens the door, I will come in to him and eat with him, and he with me."[28] Is there a contradiction here? There is no contradiction here if we understand that waiting for God in Christ is actively opening our ears to hear him knocking on the doors of our hearts. However busy we are, and however capable we are, we are reminded to listen to Christ knocking and waiting at the doors of our hearts. Revelation 3.20 also reminds us to see Christ waiting for us with those in different exiles of our times. People suffer from chattel slavery, debt bondage, forced labor, sex slavery and human trafficking, even today. Opening our hearts to Christ should also motivate us to see Christ suffering with those who suffer and extend our hand to open doors for all those who feel pain and need our help. As we wait for Christ may we also remember that He is already waiting for us.

There is a story about a rabbit born in Minnesota, a very cold place in America. It had seen only snow for many years. One day, the rabbit was taken to a warmer place and it was told that spring was coming. It thought that spring was another rabbit. The story says that after a few days, it went around asking his friends where spring was. They said, "Spring is everywhere and you are in the middle of spring."

Sadly, this is how some look for God and His comforting presence today. They don't realize that they live in the middle of God. God is all around them waiting for them if they have the eyes to see and ears to hear.

In conclusion, we need to remember that when we wait for God, we will feel the presence of Him sooner or later. Waiting for God itself is feeling the presence of God. In the next chapter, we will explore in detail the invitation of Jesus to cast our burdens unto him.

Questions for discussion and reflection

1. Do you find it easy to wait? If no, how can you develop the habit of waiting for God?
2. Trusting God is a prerequisite to wait for God patiently. If you struggle to wait for God, do you think you need to trust God more than you do now?
3. Is waiting for God an expression of our love for God?
4. Can we be so focused on the second coming of Christ and miss God in Christ coming to us at different points every

day?
5. What is the greatest gift you think God can give you?
6. How can we be "Christ" to those who wait for Him today?

5.4 Do not worry – cast your burdens unto God in Jesus in faith

It is difficult not to worry when we suffer but still here is an invitation for us to not worry. In fact, we are people who worry naturally. Understandably, we are people who become anxious of everything. In childhood, we worry about illness, childcare, health and safety. At school some worry about grades whilst others worry about not being popular. When we are grown-ups we worry about the pressure of work and job security. As we get older, we struggle with our health and we also worry about retired life. One statistic said people's worries are job, money, health, relationships, poor diet and media overload.

God in Jesus knew that we are people who worry. So, he repeatedly says do not worry.[29]

That doesn't mean that we should not be concerned about things or we should not do our best to mitigate pain and suffering. Precisely, Jesus says that the wild lilies in the mountains and wilderness grow without any human gardening. And the Greek word for consider implies to look closely, look deeply, take time and look; look at how God clothes them.

Jesus also wants us to look at the birds of the air. Certainly, we have to look at the sparrows, the blackbirds, pigeons, kites, woodpeckers and others. God feeds them. Jesus' reassuring words are, "Are you not of more value than they?"[30]

Moreover, worrying is not needed; not because we don't have needs, but because God in Jesus who made the universe asks us not to worry.

As the Bible puts it our Father in heaven, who knows what we need, loves us dearly, and is more than capable of taking good care of us. The invitation here is to move our focus away from our worry and to refocus on God.

Worry does not help

"Which of you by being anxious can add a single hour to his span of life?" asks Jesus. Worrying doesn't make things any better. Worry doesn't change the past, nor does it change the future. Jesus invites us not to worry but to trust in him.

Nothing happens to us without God's permission. If God has permitted something, He will make sure that He gets us through life. He promises to stay with us all the time.

Worry is self-centered not God-centered

When you sit in an airplane and watch the wings flap in the turbulence, it can make you worry. If you designed them, and hadn't seen this coming, you'd have good cause to be worried. But there is a team of experienced engineers who have tested everything carefully. You may not understand the physics of an aircraft wing, but you can trust them. Worrying is not keeping our eyes focused on Jesus.

When we go through the turbulence of life, we need to trust God.

In Philippians 4, Paul says that we need to stop panicking and start praying. In his words, do not worry about anything but pray about everything.

Jesus says, "Therefore I tell you, do not worry about your life, what you will eat or drink; or about your body, what you will wear. Is not life more important than food, and the body more important than clothes?"[31]

If you do an analysis of any typical women's magazine or men's magazine you will find it is preoccupied with the very things Jesus said not to worry about – clothes, food and drink. Most of the adverts focus on the body: how to shape it, how to take four-and-a-half inches off without moving an inch and how to make it more attractive. They also talk about how to look younger; how to rejuvenate your skin and make it as soft as a baby's and so on.

Jesus says that life "is more important than these things." We will miss the point of life if we always focus on ourselves rather than on God.

Cast your burdens unto God in Jesus

In India, when I was a child, I saw several platforms made of three long flat stones. Two stones worked as pillars and the third one like a platform. I knew that they were made for a purpose but I often wondered what they were for. Later, I was told what their purpose was. In Tamil they are called *Summai Thanki* which literally means "burden-bearers." In olden days, people carried huge baskets of vegetables, fruits or grains on their head and walked for miles to take them to market to sell them. Near the market place were these "weight-bearers." People would place the heavy weight that they were carrying for miles onto these and take deep breaths and relax. A feeling of relief and achievement could be seen on their faces.

Jesus says, "I am your burden bearer." "Come unto me, all you that are weary and are carrying heavy burdens, and I will give you rest."[32] The point of life is to have a relationship with God through Jesus Christ.

I should feel fortunate that there is a God and I can turn to Him. God invites us to trust Him. Your tomorrow is in God's hands.

As we saw at the beginning of this chapter, while we live in this world we are not free from burdens, struggles and problems. At times we face personal problems, health problems, problems in family and problems in our life in society. Jesus warned us that we would have problems in this world. And no one is immune to pain and no one gets to skate through life problem-free. And sometimes we happily solve one problem just to find another waiting to take its place. Not all of them are big, but most are significant in God's growth plan for us.

Nevertheless, it is a comfort to know that even righteous people like Job underwent pain. Further, "God could have kept Joseph out of jail, kept Daniel out of the lion's den, kept Jeremiah from being tossed into a slimy pit, kept Paul from being shipwrecked three times, and kept the three Hebrew young men from being thrown into the blazing furnace, but he didn't. He let those problems happen, and each of those people was drawn closer to God as a result."[33] God through those struggles – trials by fire – drew each of them more and more close to him. Just as a goldsmith watches over a furnace God carefully watches over His people. One who has triumphed over a huge tragedy or failure will find it easier to overcome smaller ordeals. That which has sprouted in fire does not wither in the sun.

The scripture says, "The Lord is close to the broken hearted; he rescues those who are crushed in spirit."[34] And as St. Peter writes we are called to cast our burdens unto Jesus because he cares for us.

As we saw earlier, Jesus says, "Come unto me all who labour and are heavy laden, and I will give you rest." Obviously, this is one of the greatest verses in the Bible. This teaching, in fact, is like a diamond, a ruby, an emerald or whatever jewel that we treasure as enormously valuable.

The background of these words of Jesus is as follows. The Jews had made religion a burden. With their numerous laws and customs, serving God had become a burden rather than a joy. For them, religion had become such a burden that they turned a blind eye to God himself. Even today, for some coming to church is a burden rather than a joy. But, for Jesus, our faith in God should bring us the greatest joy. It should turn times of struggle and pain into times of peace and hope.

People who know to cast their burdens unto Jesus are like fish in water. They swim, play and enjoy their life. But those who do not cast their burdens unto Jesus are like fish taken out of water.

Here, Jesus is offering us a tool to do our job more effectively. Jesus was creating a picture that people could understand. People could understand that he would fashion the well-fitting yoke that would make it easier to carry the loads of life.

Thus the challenge before us is, if we call ourselves Christians, and if we believe that God has revealed this truth to us, then we should live without worrying but trusting.

A typical example of a person who cast her burden unto God is Hannah, the mother of Samuel. She was carrying a burden. She didn't have children. Hannah went to church to pray for a child. She did not get a child instantly. Still, she went back in peace. She said, "I have poured out my heart to the Lord." And she went home in peace. Similarly, each time we go to church we need to pour out our heart to the Lord and go out from church, in hope, and with the power of God's peace. Each time we need to go out with some gracious and glorious promise of God. Today the promise of Jesus to you as you read this is: Cast your burdens unto me, for I care for you.

A good way to cast our burdens unto Jesus is by staying focused on God's plan, not on pains and problems. This is how Jesus endured the pain of the cross. The author of Hebrews writes, "Keep your eyes on Jesus, our leader and instructor. He was willing to die a shameful death on the cross because of the joy he knew would be his afterwards."[35] Corrie ten Boom, who suffered in a Nazi death camp, explained the power of focus: "If you look at the world, you'll be distressed. If you look within you might be depressed. But if you look at Christ you'll be at rest!"[36] We offer our burdens to Him in prayer.

Jesus not only said this but also carried our burden of sin on the cross, in our place. He has set us free. People of God are not to worry, but are called to live in that assurance, confidence, joy and hope that the Lord is the one who sets us free. "Come unto me all who labour and are heavy-laden, and I will give you rest."

It is wise to take up that generous offer.

Simple points to help you hold on to faith in God in times of pain and suffering

First, it is quite clear that denying the existence of God does not diminish our problems in any way. It is true that people are disposed to look at sufferings, sometimes more than they can bear and conclude that there is no God. But we have to be clear that that conclusion does not help in the alleviation or abolition of suffering. On the other hand, faith in God can give us the strength to bear the suffering and bring us hope that with God's grace and help things will change for the better.

Second, we need to believe that God dwells among the people and never leaves them alone. As the Psalmist puts it, even in the deepest valleys of suffering, God is there. This is what the gospel of Christ teaches us too. The love shown by Jesus Christ on the Cross affirms that God stays with us when we are afflicted. Jesus Christ, our Lord and Savior knows our pain and suffering and identifies with us when we go through them. He stays with us in times of suffering too. A true friend stays with us when we are in pain. God, our Father and True Friend, does not go away when we suffer but stays with us.

Third, we have to acknowledge that we live in a "fallen" and "broken" world. Here we must accept the simple truth that you and I sometimes suffer not because of our own mistakes, but because of others' faults too. Sometimes we are caught up in natural calamities too. In other words, suffering is part and parcel of life. No one is exempt from suffering in our far from perfect world.

Fourth, we need to learn more readily to accept that this world is no heaven and go one step further and see pain and suffering as evidence, a sort of precursor, of something better that is to come. People who put their trust in God believe that their life in this world is only a temporary one and everlasting life begins when they live with God in heaven. This acceptance helps them to hold on to their faith in God.

Fifth, whether we believe in God or not, pain is real. Both believers and non-believers go through "heaven and hell" – happy and sad experiences – in this world. Faith lends a sweet dimension to life (as they say it "adds spice" to life) and makes it worth living. Faith is therapeutic; it is an antidote to despair and depression. Faith in God promises and provides "peace that passeth all understanding."

Sixth, when we lose faith, we lose the basis of our moral values. The civilization that is built on the Christian teaching remains strong and unshaken by "storms." Christianity as a moral compass enables us to thwart the designs of the "selfish gene" and behave altruistically. One of the basic tenets of Christianity is that "We should all love our neighbors."

Seventh, I hear some people say that they wish they had a faith, something to cling onto. Perhaps they are unable to have faith in God because of their bad or bitter experiences in life. In that situation I would try to persuade them to be open-minded and seek God. In His abundant love for humanity, God promises that those who seek Him will find Him. God keeps His promises. I would here add that we should not give up until we find God. Perhaps, more precisely until God finds us.

To conclude this section, a life with faith in God is a journey undertaken with the hope of reaching the destination: "God who is our home,"[37] to quote William Wordsworth. Ups and downs are normal in this "arduous" journey and it is through ups and downs we grow in faith. The Bible invites us to trust that if God allows pain, He will give us the strength to go through it and He will show us the way out of it. We will move on to see that pain might be a temporary spiritual gift in the next sub-chapter.

Questions for discussion and reflection

1. Why should we stop worrying and start trusting?

2. Do you find it easy to refocus on your blessings and count them?

3. What can you do to let go of any burdens you carry? What does Jesus mean by saying, "Cast your burdens unto me"?

4. How can we resist taking back our burdens again after we cast them unto Jesus?

5. Did one among the seven simple points stand out for you? If yes, which one and why?

5.5 Pain might be a temporary spiritual "gift"

Anyone who says sunshine brings happiness has never danced in the rain. Life isn't about waiting for the storm to pass... it's about learning to dance in the rain. Life isn't how you survive the thunderstorm, but how you dance in the rain.

Before the time of Dr. Paul Wilson Brand, leprosy patients were thought of as people who were cursed by God. Mercifully, Brand discovered that leprosy was caused by the bacteria, *lepru bacilli*. These bacteria attacked the nerves of people. These nerves would eventually die. This meant that the leprosy patients wouldn't feel any pain in the affected area of their body. As the patients had no pain, they overused the affected area of their body. This overuse worsened the wounds. In the end the tissue became permanently damaged and fell off.

The point which Brand makes is clear. Since there was no pain in the affected area the leprosy patients couldn't react to it. They didn't know to seek help in time. They didn't have any warning that there was a problem to be sorted.

Seeing this, Brand concluded that pain is a gift from God. This is because pain alerts us to the fact that something is wrong. Pain gets our attention.

Pain is a signal to us that something is wrong and we have to do something about it.

Pain might be a call to look unto God

When children struggle in life they look unto their parents or other adults they trust for help. Children believe that the grown-ups know better and they will do all that they can to help. It is the same in other creatures. It is the instinct that is in little ones. God, our heavenly parent, wants us to know that He knows better and He is always willing to help.

In the gospels we read that people who came with their pains and struggles to Jesus found comfort and deliverance. One common thing among those who came to Jesus for comfort was that they trusted Him and asked for help. For instance, in Matthew 20:30 we read of a blind man who was told by Jesus' disciples not to shout. But he shouted, "Jesus, son of David, have mercy on me." The more he was told not to shout the more he shouted. The forces which tried to resist him calling didn't matter to him. He forgot everything except Jesus. We can follow the example of the blind man.

Pain might be a call to repent

God invites His people to live a holy life. Sometimes the pain we go through might be the result of our sinful living. If we are not sure about this, we can examine our hearts to find out if anything has gone wrong in our life. Pain and suffering can come to us if we live in sin. For example, Gehazi's greed and corruption ended in him becoming a leper.

In 2 Kings chapter 5 we read this incident. Namaan had come to the prophet Elisha to seek help. Elisha showed him, with the help of God, the way to healing. Elisha did not take any money for the help. Gehazi, Elisha's servant, was not happy with this. The Bible says,

So Gehazi hurried after Naaman. When Naaman saw Gehazi

running toward him, he got down from the chariot to meet him. "Is everything all right?" he asked. "Everything is all right," Gehazi answered. "My master sent me to say, 'Two young men from the company of the prophets have just come to me from the hill country of Ephraim. Please give them a talent of silver and two sets of clothing.'" When he went in and stood before his master, Elisha asked him, "Where have you been, Gehazi?" "Your servant didn't go anywhere," Gehazi answered. But Elisha said to him, "Was not my spirit with you when the man got down from his chariot to meet you? Is this the time to take money or to accept clothes — or olive groves and vineyards, or flocks and herds, or male and female slaves? Naaman's leprosy will cling to you and to your descendants forever." Then Gehazi went from Elisha's presence and his skin was leprous — it had become as white as snow.[38]

However, we need to bear in mind that not all illnesses or pain are caused by sin. During the time of Jesus, it was thought that any ill-health was the result of sin. Jesus made it clear that that was not the case. For Jesus, ill-health could be nothing but a means for God's glory to be revealed. Here we might also remember that even the righteous people like Job suffer. So, the idea of *karma* is not always true or straightforward.

Pain, nonetheless, is a time when we need to examine our hearts before God. If necessary, we can repent and change our ways to God's ways. The purpose of life is not just about being happy. It is also about being holy. However, holiness is, in fact, happiness in the truest and deepest sense.

Pain might be a call to depend on God

Sometimes God allows pain in our life to teach us to depend on God. When we hurt, God wants us to come to Him. Psalm 91, amongst other passages in the Bible, testifies to the fact that we can depend on God.

When we suffer, claiming God's promise to heal, we can take our struggles to God in prayer. There is no substitute to prayer in times of need and pain. We need to trust God that He hears our prayer and He is on His way to help us.

Ultimately, all suffering will end only when God's kingdom is established. Jesus asks us to pray that His kingdom will come soon so that there will be no more pain and suffering.[39]

Pain might be a test

As we noted briefly earlier, it is implicit in the Book of Job that the suffering he has to undergo in life, is actually a test for him. It is a test to prove whether he continues to trust God even in his immense and unbearable pain. Job is steadfast in his faith in God. No amount of suffering could make him turn away from God. He treats suffering as part of life. His firm belief is that we who have enjoyed abundance in the hands of God have to undergo suffering with equanimity. Finally, he emerges a winner. We too, in times of test, are called to have unshaken faith in God, like Job.

Pain might be a time when we know the love of God in its fullness

A person who has gone through deep agony and suffering understands the emotions of another person's suffering better. God in Jesus experienced the most agonizing pain on Maundy Thursday and Good Friday. This tells us that God knows our pain. He has the experience of being a human in Jesus. God empathizes with us during our troubles and pains.

It is not always easy to feel that we are God-filled, especially at difficult times, but we are invited to trust the presence of God with us even in the deepest valleys of suffering.

We can tell God, "I don't understand this but I trust that you are with me." Jesus realized that even though He felt forsaken on the cross, God the Father was still with Him. That is why he calls out, "My God, my God, you have forsaken me?" That is why He commits his spirit into the hands of the Father. It affirms that Jesus knew that God the Father was close to Him and the Father could still hear Him cry. This gives us the wisdom and knowledge to call out to God in our pain knowing that God hears our cries, sees our tears and listens to our prayers.

The one who understands our pain and stays with us during pain is our real friend. A true friend loves us more than him/herself. Pain is a time when we need to look for God's presence with us and know His love. Pain puts things in perspective. God in Jesus participates in our pain. Such is His love for us.

Pain might be an invitation to know that God in Jesus stays with us when we struggle

Matthew, Mark and Luke tell us the story of Jesus staying in the boat when the disciples were in danger. They say that one day Jesus got into a boat, at the sea of Galilee, and said to his disciples, "Let us go across to the other side." The disciples followed him into the boat. When they were sailing there arose a great storm on the sea and Jesus was asleep. The disciples remembered to wake him. Jesus woke up and rebuked the winds and the sea; and there was great calm again.

Even today, Christ calls us to experience this wonder and amazement, in Him, in all storms of life. At times, when Jesus was surrounded by the dangers created by the Pharisees and the Sadducees He disappeared and went away. However, when He was with His disciples during the great storm he continued to stay with them. For God's people, great storms and perils may come. But Jesus remains a hope, a comfort and a strength for those who put their complete trust in Him. He never leaves them to fend for themselves.

Our call in life is to live a God-led life every day. Our trust indeed needs to be in God. I am convinced that, when I trust

God, live a life of repentance and follow God in Christ, even if I end up in hell for some reason, God will still be with me.

Pain might be an invitation to focus on the long term

Our life in this world is a journey towards oneness with God. During this journey pain and suffering are inevitable. It is not just a few but everyone undergoes pain at one time or another. But it is important for us to know that God uses this time to transform His people and draw them more and more close to him. Perhaps, God even permits trials to help His people gain confidence in Him. I sometimes think pains and struggles are more for those who live close to God. However, God is careful to comfort and deliver them from the struggles. Pain ultimately is an invitation to look beyond the things we see in this world to the things we don't see but are promised in the next world.

As Paul says, "For this light momentary affliction is preparing for us an eternal weight of glory beyond all comparison, as we look not to the things that are seen but to the things that are unseen. For the things that are seen are transient, but the things that are unseen are eternal."[40]

Matthew, amongst others, reminds us that our God calls us to go across to "the other side." Life is a long journey of going across to the other side by which I mean heaven. According to Matthew, what is certain is those who journey with Jesus are sure to reach across the other side safely. The good news is that it is not mere hope but that God, through His scripture, gives us the assurance and confidence that His ways for us are higher and wiser than our own ways for ourselves. Our life on this earth is just the dress rehearsal before the real production. God calls us to journey with Him to reach the other side safely.

Jesus conquered the world, the sea, the depths, the heights and even death through His death on the cross and his resurrection. This is where we have the assurance and confidence of reaching across the "other side" safely. We will look at this in detail in the next chapter.

Questions for discussion or reflection

1. Do you agree that pain sometimes can be a blessing in disguise?

2. Do you naturally turn to God when a difficulty comes into your life? If no, what stops you?

3. Repentance is a significant theme in the Bible. How important do you think regular self-examination and repentance are?

4. Has any suffering in life forced you to believe that you need God?

5. Jesus identifies with us by going through pain and suffering on the cross. Do you find this a comforting thought?

6. Do you think the existence of pain in our broken world is a pointer to a better world to come?

Chapter 6

Life Is Temporary— Created to Discover the Permanent Life

6.1 Assurance of life beyond death

If the world hates you, keep in mind that it hated me first. If you belonged to the world, it would love you as its own. As it is, you do not belong to the world, but I have chosen you out of the world. That is why the world hates you.[1]

My Father's house has many rooms; if that were not so, would I have told you that I am going there to prepare a place for you? And if I go and prepare a place for you, I will come back and take you to be with me that you also may be where I am.[2]

In the last chapter, we looked at tackling the problem of suffering from different angles, with the help of God. In this final chapter, we will explore the dimension of eternal life and ways to prepare for it. We are created by God not just to enjoy glimpses of His presence in the world around us but also to discover and ponder on the glorious future He has prepared for His people. The light and beauty, and joy of what is to come, according to the scripture, are matchless.

I often wonder why we put so much effort, energy, time and resources into making our transient and temporary, and relatively short life in this world, "successful" and why we don't take a bit more time to enjoy exploring the joys of everlasting life that God in Jesus has prepared for us. Of course, we need to be doing all that we can in creating a better world here and now and for the generations to come but I sometimes wonder if we have got the balance right.

One reason why many do not ponder on the life to come could be that they are not quite sure about the existence of everlasting life. Here are three reasons to be certain about it.

First, God in Jesus Christ has made it clear to us that His Kingdom is not of this world. God's Kingdom is where God's rule prevails. Jesus even promises that He is going to prepare a place for us. His father's house has many rooms. And He will come again to take us to be with himself. Some have argued that eternal life in God's presence must be a boring or monotonous one because we will just be singing hallelujahs all the time. John Polkinghorne, a physicist and theologian says, the reference to many rooms by Jesus "is not one of a celestial hotel with everything laid on – 'This is your room!' – but of a process. It means there are many 'stages', and all these 'stages' will be open to us ... it is the unending exploration of the reality of God, progressively unveiled, that seems to me to be behind this image translated in the Authorised Version as 'mansions'. That seems to me the most persuasive picture of the life to come."[4] Eternal exploration of the joy and wonder of God will be fascinating indeed.

No doubt, whatever interpretation we want to hold on to, this passage is most popular at funeral services, and it regularly brings comfort, peace and hope to the bereaved family. However, this passage should really help us to get our perspective right throughout our life in this world and not just at funeral services. Most of the problems that stem from the negative side of human nature can be addressed if we come to understand that we are all created for eternity and we are all equal before God. God-inspired life invites us to see the big picture that God has in mind beyond time, space and our relatively short life in this world.

Second, billions and billions of people for many centuries, who have gone before us, believed that there was more – more than life in this world. Our meaning and purpose should be discerned in the light of eternity. Many men and women have seen visions of heaven both in the Bible and in the history of religions. For instance, the well-known Psalm 23 ends with the words, "I will dwell in the house of the Lord forever." Scripture even talks about Enoch and Elijah and later Jesus being taken to the heavens with their body. People of faith in the Judeo-Christian tradition and other faiths for thousands of years have believed that there is more to life than the short life we live now. Surely, what those billions understood cannot be wrong? We go for the product with the most reviews on Amazon and in other shops. Shouldn't we trust the witnesses and experiences of billions of people who have lived and died before us rather than classifying all of them as hallucinations?

Third, even if we apply reason to the notion of eternal life it is only logical to think that there is more. If we take the view that this life is all that there is, what is the point of life? We are born, we grow, and generally speaking, we get a job and make some money, we get old and die. Moreover, many die at a young age too. Isn't it? The question of meaning and purpose is not answered in a satisfactory manner in this view. But, if you take the eternal perspective of life, life in this world can be seen as a time that we take to get closer to God with whom we will spend all eternity.

The use of miracle stories today

Similar to today, there were people with problems in mind, body and spirit while Jesus lived. For example, a leper told Jesus, "Lord, if you choose, you can make me clean." We can imagine how much he would have wept and how much pain he would have had both physically and emotionally. He came and knelt before Jesus and prayed to Him. Jesus healed him. This is just one among the many miracles we read in the Bible.

What could this miracle and other miracles mean to us today? The miracles of Jesus encourage us and give us confidence to talk about the relief we could find in God in Jesus and the hope we have in him always. We know that miracles happen even today and they happen in God's time and in His ways. I believe that for God's people He brings a happy ending in some way.

In fact, we can hold on to the passages that deal with miracles and pray for relief in times of need. Miracles, in John's Gospel, are seen as signs of God's Kingdom. And those signs can be revealed in us, for us and through us too.

Miracle stories remind us that nothing is impossible with God. They are invitations to hold on to God in faith and hope. They are signs that point to the fact that there is more. In other words, they are glimpses of heaven on earth. Perhaps the greatest miracle is God in Christ raising people from the dead. We will briefly look at Jesus raising Lazarus from the dead.

Jesus raises Lazarus from the dead: John's point of view

Whenever we read St. John's Gospel, the echo we can hear in the background is life in its fullness or life eternal or life in Christ. That is the central theme of John. Jesus raising Lazarus from the dead is where we see John's pivotal portrayal of what is possible with God.

What does John make out of this incident? What does he really want to tell his readers? Obviously, this is a miracle story. But for John a miracle is much more than that because it has eternal significance. For John, a miracle is a "sign" of the revelation of God's glory. What does he mean by that? Precisely, for him, a miracle is not just a unique event at one point in time but it is something that points to the eternal sovereignty and providence of God. In relation to the raising of Lazarus, John would say that Jesus at Bethany was not just raising Lazarus from the dead but was also showing us that that is what would happen to all of us one day. God has the power to raise people from the dead.

A good example of understanding John's thinking is to remember the first miracle that he records. It is Jesus changing water into wine at Cana. John doesn't tell us, oh, that is a miracle, but he says that was the first sign through which Jesus revealed his glory.

John says, "Jesus asked Martha, 'Do you believe that I am the resurrection and life?' Martha says, 'Yes, Lord I believe.'" Jesus reveals that he is the resurrection and life. He reveals that our lives come from Him and new life is possible with Him even beyond death.

So, John is simply teaching us that this is what will happen to all of us one day – and we will meet all who have gone before us – including Lazarus. Whether we like it or not, we will face our friends and beloved ones and we will also face those with whom we were not on very friendly terms with in this worldly life. Not to worry, all will be transformed. Once in heaven, people of God will be happy to see those who they might not otherwise wish to see. It will be a transformation into a new life. And, significantly, we people of God, will get the greatest joy when we face God in Jesus directly on that day. Lazarus raising from the dead is a sign of Jesus' authority over our lives.

Overcome fear of death: Moral of the story

What would Lazarus have made of his own resurrection? A few years ago, I read a play by Eugene O'Neill titled, *Lazarus Laughed*. I was moved when reading the play because Eugene has really underlined the significance of the raising of Lazarus to life from Lazarus' perspective.

The play actually begins where the biblical story ends. As the curtain goes up, Lazarus is seen stumbling out of the dark, blinking into the sunlight. He embraces Jesus with gratitude and he begins to talk to his sisters. But people interrupt. Obviously, they want to know what happened when he died. And some boldly ask, "Don't test our patience, Lazarus, tell us what it's like to die. What lies on the other side of this boundary that none of us have crossed?"

At that point, Lazarus began to laugh loudly and he said, "You won't believe me – but I tell you the truth – there is no death, really. There is only life. There is only God. There is only incredible joy."

He continued, "Death is not the way it appears from this side. But it is a portal through which we move into everlasting growth and everlasting life. There is nothing to be fearful about." And in that play, he appears to be a person who doesn't fear death.

Not everyone in Bethany was pleased with this turn of events. And the Roman authorities were quick to sense that Lazarus was a threat to their authority. At the end he stands face to face with the Roman emperor, the most powerful person of all on earth. He says to Lazarus, "Deny Jesus or I will put you to death." Lazarus laughs and says, "There is no death really, there is only life."

The emperor is confused because he has never met a person raised from the dead and who does not fear death. Lazarus appears more powerful because he doesn't fear. That's how the play ends.

The scripture very frequently says fear not. It doesn't fail to tell us very often do not be afraid. Lazarus raising from the dead teaches us not to be afraid – for those who put their trust in God there is only life.

Encourage one another in hope

Paul says, Brothers and sisters, we do not want you to be uninformed about those who sleep in death, so that you do not grieve like the rest of mankind, who have no hope. For we believe that Jesus died and rose again, and so we believe that God will bring with Jesus those who have fallen asleep in him. According to the Lord's word, we tell you that we who are still alive, who are left until the coming of the Lord, will certainly not precede those who have fallen asleep. For the Lord himself will come down from heaven, with a loud

*command, with the voice of the archangel and with the trumpet call
of God, and the dead in Christ will rise first. After that, we who are
still alive and are left will be caught up together with them in the
clouds to meet the Lord in the air. And so we will be with the Lord
forever. Therefore encourage one another with these words.*[5]

In the gospels, not only do we read about Jesus raising Lazarus
from the dead but also that Jesus raised a widow's son. In another
place we read that Jesus raised a little girl. However, we don't
see people raising from the dead nowadays. But I think that is
why we need to encourage one another in hope. To those who
have lost their brother or sister – we are called to be a brother
or a sister, to those who have lost their children we are called
be children and love them as children love their parents and to
those who have lost their friend, we can be their friend. People
cry because when they lose someone – they know that they are
not there to receive their love.

But we are here to offer hope, and to comfort one another
with no fear of death because we are indeed here and now to
discover that there is more. Death is just going home, nothing to
be afraid of. As Paul says we don't grieve without hope.

To conclude this section, heaven is not just a gift we receive
from God when we die. Heaven is something that should bring
joy and strength to us now, to live purposefully, in the present.
One of the purposes of this life is to discover the joy of permanent
life in hope and trust. In the next sub-chapter, we will examine
the resurrection of Jesus himself and its implications on our life
today.

Questions for reflection or discussion

1. Do you find the concept of permanent life with God
   liberating from the fear of this being the only life we have?
2. When people go on a holiday they generally plan a lot
   for it. However, why do you think many are reluctant to

ponder on the concept of everlasting life?

3. Do you think it is important to talk about eternal life? And why?

4. Does the assurance of eternal life for all those who believe in God in Jesus encourage you to live a faithful life now?

5. John calls miracles "signs." Do you find this helpful to understand the miracles of Jesus?

6. Some Bible scholars suggest that Lazarus raising from the dead is more or less restored to life (because he died again) and Jesus' resurrection is a very different kind (because he will never die again). Do you find this distinction helpful or not?

7. Do you think faith in God drives away the fear of death?

6.2 Jesus' Resurrection-inspired life

Jesus' resurrection points us to a new way of looking at the world, a new way of being that changes who we are and how we live in the world

(Paula Gooder)[6]

The good news of Jesus' resurrection is that in Christ, darkness, destruction and even death are never the end of the story. The darkness giving way to the light of the presence of angels, as happened on Easter Day, is the turning point of many of our life experiences.

Living in the light of the resurrection of Jesus is not to move backwards. It is not even to remain static. The resurrection of Jesus inspires us to move forward.

For the Israelites, the Exodus was arguably the most joyous event. In fact, it was an experience of resurrection to them. The Egyptians were following the Israelites to capture them and ahead of the Israelites was the Red Sea. They found no way to move forward. In many ways, we find ourselves in a similar situation even today. We struggle to move forward amidst the confusions and anxieties caused by the exclusive scientific approach to life, forces of secularism, agnosticism, certain apathy about godly living in our society and internal problems of the church itself. Often, we grumble without clarity. In the Exodus event too, the Israelites began to grumble. They said to Moses, "It would have been better for us to serve the Egyptians than to die in this wilderness." In this situation of apprehension, it is significant to see what God said to Moses: "Tell the Israelites to move forward."[7] Notably, in this Old Testament incident God leads them, through the darkness, with the aid of a pillar of fire. Some biblical scholars suggest that the pillar of fire refers to an ancient active volcano. However, the point is that the Israelites knew that God was leading them in some way. Even today, God calls you and me to move forward realizing the presence of the light of the risen Jesus leading us. Just as God led the Israelites, through the darkness, with the aid of a pillar of fire, He wishes to lead His people in the light, joy, wonder and the power of the resurrection.

Similar to the exodus event, the prophet Isaiah spoke about Judah's song of victory. Isaiah says, "Open the gates, so that the righteous nation that keeps faith may enter in."[8] Here too, the message of God delivering His people from exile, a situation similar to that of the dead, is not the end in itself. The message of deliverance is a message of forward movement.

New understanding of God

Easter is a message of victory, from which we can gain enormous inspiration. You might know that the church itself, as we know it today, was born out of the evidence of Jesus' resurrection. In fact, the resurrection of Jesus provides a new understanding of God allowing you and me to move forward. The New Understanding of God is that God who heals memories of shame, injury, guilt, sin and its effects is also a God with whom a new relationship is possible through the risen Lord. St. Paul says that it is because Jesus died for our sins and because God raised him from the dead that a new union with God is possible.[9] You and I can now move forward because we have this unique message of a new relationship that is possible with God in and through the risen Jesus.

New understanding of life

Along with a new understanding of God, the resurrection of Jesus brings us a new understanding of life. Again, as Paul says to the Romans, we die with Christ for our sins and rise with Him for a new life. He goes on to say that it is because we rise with Christ for a new life, sin must no longer rule us but God must rule us for righteous purposes.[10] The dying and rising of Christ affirms that we no longer live under law but under God's grace. Thus, the message of the church, which witnesses the risen Lord, is that no one should any longer live in sin but should have a new life in union with God. For Paul, when we lead a new life in union with God, sin cannot reign over us.

Sometimes people are reluctant to be inspired in their Christian life, because they are not sure if the resurrection message is worthy enough to be celebrated and shared. I believe that there can be no greater message than the resurrection message – if rightly understood – to lead anyone towards a transformed and new life.

The witness of Mary Magdalene

Mary was distressed and was in despair following the crucifixion of Jesus. The one person who gave meaning to her life had died on the cross. She was denied performing her last loving service of anointing his dead body with spices and aromatic oils because the body of Jesus had disappeared. She wept her heart out. On peering into the tomb, she saw angels who tried to tell her that this was no time for weeping: she was looking in the wrong place. Some in our society do that too – looking for comfort in alcoholism, drugs and other things instead of God in Jesus.

The story takes a twist at last. Jesus rose from the dead. He called her name, Mary. She cried out, "My Master and My Teacher." Excited with the encounter she went and told the disciples. "I have seen the Lord."[11] Mary was then at peace. She met the risen Jesus. She was transformed. She became a source of inspiration.

The witness of other women

It is worth noting how the resurrection inspired people around Jesus to move forward. Not only Mary Magdalene but a few other women also went with the spices they prepared to do the final anointing to Jesus' body. This portrayed that no one expected Jesus would rise again. It was still dark in the morning, but the stone was rolled away from the tomb. When they went in, they did not find the body. But two men appeared in dazzling clothes and said to them, "Why do you look for the living among the dead? He is not here, he has risen."[12]

Luke tells his readers that the women returned and told the eleven disciples all that had happened.[13] They could no longer wait – they moved forward with the good news of the resurrection. Interestingly, it is the resurrection of Jesus which inspired the gospel writers to record the good news as we have them today.

The resurrection of Christ should encourage us and inspire us to live a God-inspired life every day. The New Testament evidence of Easter should be co-related with our present experience of the risen Christ. It is when we die for our sins and rise with Christ for a new life and make the resurrection experience our own that we will live differently.

Witness of the disciples: Evidence of the resurrection

The disciples were full of fear even though it was the very day of the resurrection. And further Mary had given her lovely testimony – but still fear had not left them. In the evening of that day, the first day of the week, the doors being shut where the disciples were, for fear of the Jews. They had to grapple with the "what next" question. Sometimes we too can be filled with fear. The disciples were afraid so they shut the doors, and they sat inside the house, thoroughly frozen!

And remember this is not anti-Semitism – the disciples were Jews themselves! Fear turned their kith and kin into enemies to be feared. We too might be placed in similar situations. Nonetheless, just as Jesus came to Mary, he came to the disciples too. The doors were completely shut. No one was expected to come in. Sometimes we too feel no one should step into our life. So we shut every door carefully, bolts and everything; we turn the key in the lock and we sit in that prison of "security." The recent Covid-19 pandemic gave many of us a flavor of this "staying at home" experience. Nevertheless, Jesus still came in. You don't know how he came in – you look around and look at him – there he is. Jesus came and stood among them. And he said to them – Peace be with you.

The attitude of the disciples changed completely after they saw the risen Jesus. From Peter to John, the beloved disciple of Christ, they were a sad collection of broken and frightened people. The fear was rational but immobilising. Jesus' resurrection changed them into bold witnesses who turned the world upside down by their testimony to the triumph of God's love in Jesus. The disciples moved forward – from sadness to joy, from fear to courage, from doubt to certainty and from darkness to light. They began to think bold. In those days, each one of them went to different parts of the world to witness Jesus and carry out his mission. Following the resurrection, those who denied Jesus started witnessing and those who said no suffering should come upon Jesus themselves were then prepared to suffer for him. Peter says, "You disowned the Holy and the Righteous

One and asked that a murderer be released to you. You killed the author of life, but God raised him from the dead. We are witnesses of this."[14] Before the council, he also says we cannot but proclaim the good news. The immense change in the attitude of the disciples is evidence of the resurrection.

You can listen to the testimony of the previously frightened disciples. St. John writes, "The disciples were overjoyed when they saw the Lord."[15] What about their fear? It had been taken care of. The resurrection of Jesus Christ is the guarantee of our joy, the passport which we can hold firmly and say, weak as I am, because he rose from the dead and left my fears in the grave, I can now walk as a loved child of God. Jesus Christ's resurrection assures us of God's help to know his presence, forgiveness, joy and peace.

It is when we believe the incredible event of resurrection, we gain strength and inspiration to live differently. We may go forward by way of our participation in church activities, the time we give to teach the scripture to ourselves, our friends, our children and grandchildren and the time we spend with God in prayer. We may live Christianly, differently and purposefully and move forward. It is when all of us move forward that communities and societies will be changed for the better. Christ had to be risen for each one of us and He did rise. Belief that Jesus rose on the third day must be based more on encountering Christ in our experiences than in the discovery of the empty tomb. It is important to make Jesus' resurrection a real experience in our day-to-day life.

The revelation on the way to Emmaus

Jesus met two of the confused disciples on the road to Emmaus. They discussed the events of Good Friday but got nowhere. They were disappointed and disorientated.

Jesus joined them and they treated him as a stranger in Jerusalem. As he spoke, their hearts burned within them but their eyes remained closed because of their utter confusion and disappointment. But as Jesus broke bread, they caught sight of the familiar act, and their hearts were liberated from self-doubt and despair.

They went wounded in their spirit. They returned with excitement to Jerusalem. They went with confused news: they returned with good news. They went to Emmaus in blindness: they returned with a clear vision of Jesus Christ. That's what the risen Christ did for them. He drove out their doubt and lifted their spirits.

Clearly, we need God's help to fulfill His wishes and to respond to the needs of others; and to become caring, loving and joyous people. It is in God that we find our fulfillment in its true sense. We can set great store by God's assurance that He will one day transform this decaying, dying and imperfect world into a completely new world.

The resurrection of Jesus as evidence of our own resurrection

We can live a God-led life with energy, purpose and joy because Jesus' resurrection is a presage of our own resurrection. The resurrection of Jesus reminds us that death is not the end; it doesn't have the last say. This is why Christians call themselves Easter people. The resurrection is the power of God revealed in Jesus in the midst of death, the ultimate enemy. This means we are to live in hope, not just hope for the resurrection life which God offers to His people even beyond "death," but the hope of the risen Christ bringing a foretaste of the new life into our everyday lives here and now. Nothing, in my view, can be more powerful than the resurrection of Jesus to motivate, inspire and uplift us to move forward and live differently. Having reflected on Jesus' resurrection and its meaning in this sub-chapter, we will move on to describe the qualities of heaven and its implications for living a God-inspired life today.

Questions for reflection or discussion

1. Is the Book of Exodus relevant for our times? What kind of exodus experience do you think our communities need today?

2. Do you think Christian understanding of God is different to other major religions? If yes, in what ways? And does the resurrection have an impact?

3. What impact does the resurrection have in our society's life and culture?

4. What are the similarities and differences between "living under law" and "living under grace"?

5. In what ways does Jesus' resurrection inspire you to live differently?

6. Do you consider the testimony of Mary and the other women to be good evidences of the resurrection?

7. The Risen Jesus came to His disciples when they were frightened, saddened and confused. Do you believe that the Risen Jesus comes to us even today when we face difficult situations? If yes, can you give an example?

8. Have you had Emmaus Road experiences in your life?

6.3 Pondering on heaven to live purposefully on earth

God has planted eternity in the human heart.[16]

Live for God until your last breadth. This will certainly help with a smooth transition to your real home.
(Billy Graham)

Death is real. It is part of life but it changes everything. No one is exempt from it. Hopefully, it is not too soon, but one day your life and mine in this world will come to an end. For Paul, death is the last enemy.[17] For people of God, life after death is more real than life before death. But why should we learn about heaven?

We learn about heaven to live life in the light of heaven now. We learn about heaven to live Christianly, differently, fulfillingly and purposefully here on earth.

As we saw earlier, the good news is that we are created not just for this life and not just for this world but also for a completely new life and for a totally new world that is to come. For all people of God, heaven is their home. Heaven will be greater than the sweetest and wildest dream humanity could ever have. I am convinced that this is the case. We have to live for Jesus in this world until Jesus' preparation is completely over for us.

However, it is a fact that many people do not believe in the existence of heaven or hell today. Now and then I come across people in my village community who say that there is nothing more after we die. In their words, death is death. Some others say that life after death is just a lovely thought. They say that they hope that there is more but they don't really believe in it. I do feel sad when people say this because they haven't yet realized that there is more in us than flesh and bones. We have a spirit or a soul or a quintessence or an epitome within us. Teilhard says, "We are not human beings having a spiritual experience. We are spiritual beings having a human experience."[18] We are created to live eternally. As King Solomon says God has set eternity in the hearts of people.

In the practical sense John quotes the words of Jesus, "My Father's house has many rooms, if that were not so, would I have told you that I am going there to prepare a place for you? And if I go and prepare a place for you, I will come back and take you to be with me that you also may be where I am."[19] Jesus not only said this but died and rose again to reassure us with the greatest good news that there is more; death is not the end but the beginning of a new and better life. There is an on-going discussion on whether heaven is a different place or will heaven come on this very earth we live one day. It really doesn't matter which view you hold, what matters is to take the invitation by

God in Jesus to be in His direct presence eternally.

Now, what will heaven be like. If we are to prepare for a life with God in heaven, we need to have some idea of it. Otherwise, how would we prepare.

Every August I go to India for a holiday. India is also the country where I grew up as a child. It doesn't matter which month it is but whenever I think of the next holiday in my place of birth in India, I become joyous and excited. This is because I know what to expect. I know that the weather will be perfect for me, I know the landscapes, I know the culture and I know that I will meet my wider family and friends in India. The thought of going there for a holiday makes me happy.

In the long term heaven is our eternal home. We can rejoice in this life because one of the purposes of this life is to prepare for the next. We will see more about preparation in the next sub-chapter but here we move on to see what the Bible has to say about what heaven is not and what heaven is.

What heaven is not?

First, absence of God is not heaven but hell. Hell is taking things for granted. In other words, God is not in the picture. On the other hand, heaven is not taking things for granted. It is opening our eyes to see glimpses of God and His heavenly goodness around us and giving thanks for them every day.

Second, heaven is not a world where injustice, poverty, violence, jealousy, greed and other evil things exist. If we look around the world – and our own countries – we see so much injustice even today. For example, child labor, human trafficking, homelessness, misuse of power, greed, the poor struggling for a meal a day – are realities of our world. These are glimpses of hell.

Third, heaven is not about illness, brokenness or death. You might know the words used by Canon Henry Holland in St. Paul's Cathedral on Whitsunday 1910, reflecting on the passing of King Edward VII. "Death is nothing at all. I have only slipped away into the next room." These were certainly words of comfort and kind words but we do miss our loved ones when they leave us. Well, no one dies in heaven. Moreover, there are no physical restrictions or space and time constraints.

So, what precisely is heaven?
Heaven is the home of God

The Bible repeatedly tells us that God dwells in heaven, which precisely means heaven is God's home. For example, the scripture says, "Look down from your holy habitation, from heaven, and bless your people Israel and the ground that you have given us, as you swore to our fathers, a land flowing with milk and honey."[20] The good news is God's invitation to his home is open to us all. Practicing living a life with God now is the best way to live life not only now but eternally. Indeed, as Billy Graham says, living for God now will help with a smooth transition to everlasting life with God in heaven.

Heaven is about worship

Biblically, the significant thing about heaven is worship. It's no coincidence that one scriptural picture of heaven is of singing, because singing together is a wonderful illustration of what it means to have a body of your own but to find your true voice in a much greater body. Singing praises to God with others is what will happen in heaven. Worshipful singing is finding your voice most fully in words of praise and thanksgiving. You rejoice at the gifts of others which only enhance the gifts that are yours. This is the reason why many churches have choirs. Music can draw you closer to God. Music and singing performed to praise God can lift you closer to God.

Every Sunday Christians gather together and contemplate the life to come. That's why worship matters so much – because in eternity, worship is spontaneous. And worship isn't just some abstract ideal. Worship is not only edifying for life here and now but it is also preparing to live a life in the direct presence of God.

The Book of Revelation makes it absolutely clear who we worship – we worship the Lamb who was slain, the Lamb on the throne, Jesus, the one who gave his life. What we strive for in worship is to focus that every bit of our energy and concentration on the God we find in Jesus Christ so that we are truly lost in wonder, love and praise – because that's what heaven is like. We can have breathtaking heavenly moments on earth but heaven is where we will fully and truly be ourselves.

Heaven is about friendship

Friendship is what heaven is about – not just between God and us but also friendship between one another. Living together as friends is at the heart of heaven, just as worship is. The reason why Christian communities work hard at their relationships with their neighborhoods, villages, towns and cities as they do at their worship is that they believe making friendships across social barriers is what they shall spend eternity doing, and what they are called to do now is to anticipate heaven. St. Augustine said, "We have not lost our dear ones who have departed from this life, but have merely sent them ahead of us, so we also shall depart and shall come to that life where they will be more than ever dear as they will be better known to us, and where we shall love them without fear of parting." He also said, "All of us who enjoy God are also enjoying each other in Him."[21]

Learning that heaven is about friendship should motivate us to make friends. It should also encourage us to keep in touch with friends. When we build, cherish and enjoy friendship here on earth today, we live in the light of heaven.

Heaven is about eating together

This is not because all of us enjoy good food but because this is the most common picture of heaven in the New Testament –

heaven as a great feast, a banquet celebrating the marriage of heaven and earth, the perfect union or communion of God and all God's children. Just imagine a fabulous meal where there were no allergies, no eating disorders, no fatty foods and no price tag.

The reason why the Eucharist is at the center of the life of the Church is because the Eucharist is where food, friendship and worship all come together. Jesus says that He is the bread of heaven. When we partake the meal of Eucharist, our spiritual taste buds, in faith, need to foretaste the food of heaven given to us in advance.

Heaven is about glory

People sometimes talk about a glorious sunrise or sunset or waterfall or a tall mountain. However, the most glorious things in this world wouldn't be comparable to the glory of heaven. The Book of Revelation talks about the glory of heaven. John writes, heaven's "brilliance was like that of a very precious jewel, like a jasper, clear as crystal."[22] Heaven "does not need the sun or the moon to shine on it, for the glory of God gives it light, and the Lamb is its lamp."[23] We can see John feeling the inadequacy of human language to explain the beauty of heaven.

Most importantly, God is ever present in heaven. The presence of God in His fullness is heaven's greatest beauty. I can't begin to imagine how much more beautiful would a place be when God in Jesus Himself prepares it. No wonder, Paul writes that he can't wait to behold this beauty with his own eyes. But for now, we have to fulfill our purposes for which God has kept us in this world. Pondering on heaven is to let God work in us and through us now. When we offer ourselves into God's hands, we begin to do our best.

Heaven is about newness

In the last chapter we looked at the suffering in this world. In heaven, there is no sin, no evil, no suffering and so there will be no more tears. God will wipe away all tears if any at all.[24] Life with only tears of joy will be new for us.

Heaven is about joy

The greatest joy of heaven will be meeting God in Jesus as He actually is. "You make known to me the path of life; in your presence there is fullness of joy; at your right hand are pleasures forevermore."[25]

We will meet our loved ones who have gone before us. Meeting my granddad again in his new and pain-free body is something I look forward to. I want to ask him what made him the faithful, committed, kindest and loveliest person he actually was.

According to Paul, we now see through a veil but then we will see everything as they actually are. In his words, "Now we see things imperfectly, like puzzling reflections in a mirror, but then we will see everything with perfect clarity. All that I know now is partial and incomplete, but then I will know everything completely, just as God now knows me completely."[26]

Heaven is about going home

As they say, home is home. Home is a place of security, comfort and peace. It doesn't matter where we live on this planet nothing is certain, no place is safe and nothing works perfectly in this world. I will dwell in the house of the Lord forever, says the psalmist. Rejoice, every day we take one step closer to our real home. In fact, belief in eternal and everlasting life should indeed change the way we see ourselves, others, the world we live in and it should fine-tune our lives for the better.

Heaven is heaven – What now?

The fullness of heavenly existence although is in the future, pondering on heaven is a joyous thing to do. This is not escapism from the present realities, but it is about living differently, purposefully and hopefully in the light of heaven now.

Pondering on heaven teaches us that we don't have to fulfill all of the things on our bucket list in this short life. There is eternity. This will help us to do fewer things but with clear purpose and to do them well. This can help us relax and enjoy life today rather than worry about the endless things on our to-do list.

To conclude, heaven reminds us of who God is. It reminds us of God's creative power and His readiness to open up His home for you and me. Pondering on heaven should lead us to commit to live a God-inspired life today for there is no other life better than that.

Heaven reminds us of who we really are too – mere mortals but called for a rich inheritance. You and I are far more valuable, in God, than we often think.

Pondering on heaven should not only transform the way we do things but also change the attitude with which we live our everyday lives. In the next section, we will reflect on the joy and excitement of our preparation to be in God's direct presence eternally.

Questions for reflection or discussion

1. Is the promise of life with God in heaven for those who trust in God in Jesus, when their time here is over, comforting?

2. How can we practice living in relationship with God now? What are the common obstacles people face?

3. Do you believe that when we worship God, we join in with the all the angelic hosts of heaven? If yes, how should we worship?

4. How would you explain the glory of heaven to a friend who asks you?

5. Is there a difference between heavenly joy and worldly

joy? If yes, can you say it in a few words?

6. Why do we sometimes struggle to submit to God's vision for our life?

6.4 Rejoice in your preparation

Job said, Naked I came from my mother's womb, and naked shall I return there; the Lord gave, and the Lord has taken away; blessed be the name of the Lord.[27]

The ultimate purpose of this life is to prepare to meet God face to face in His heavenly home.

Of course, while we live in this world, we have many ambitions in our lives. Children who are at schools and universities will want to do well in their exams. Those of us who are involved with various jobs and who work in different capacities will want to carry out our responsibilities well. Retired people too would have many things to do which they might not have been able to do while they were working. However, even while we are involved in the many works at our home and in our society, we should not forget that we ought to prepare ourselves to meet God face to face. After all, our life this side of eternity is temporary, what is permanent is yet to come. As the psalmist says,

As for mortals, their days are like grass; they flourish like a flower of the field; for the wind passes over it, and it is gone, and its place knows it no more. But the steadfast love of the Lord is from everlasting to everlasting on those who fear him, and his righteousness to children's children.[28]

Suppose you have good friends in a different town or country and you are going to see them. How would you prepare? You would start preparing for the travel. You may also think about the things you need to take with you, what are the things you need to share with your friends and so on? You might also think about insurance. If you have a dog or a cat you will have to arrange for someone to look after them in your absence. There is a joy in preparing for exciting things of the future. And similarly, there is a joy in preparing ourselves to meet God fearfully and carefully. Perhaps that is the greatest preparation that we need to do in our lives. How do we do that?

As we saw briefly in the preface, there was a rich man who once asked Jesus, "What must I do to be saved."[29] Jesus said, "Obey the commandments, you shall not murder, you shall not commit adultery, you shall not steal, you shall not defraud; honour your father and mother." So, the first step is to get away from evil and selfish desires of our hearts and obey God's commandments. Many of the saintly people of God in the past actually had plenty of choices in their life. Some of them were well learned, educated and rich people materially. But they chose to let go of any selfish desires and dedicated themselves to live a God-inspired life day after day. What are my priorities? What are your priorities? Preparing to meet God is first of all about getting our priorities right. Living a God-inspired life should be our first priority. This will happen when we realize the Majesty and Holiness of Christ and also realize our limitations without God.

The rich man said that he had kept all the commandments. Jesus continued, "One more thing – go, sell what you own and give the money to the poor and then follow me." He got a shock and went away. My granddad used to say, "In the gospels many people came to Jesus for help. Some came with their questions. All who came for help went away rejoicing except this man. Why? He had the heart only to serve money but not to serve God. Watch out." Preparing for a life with God in heaven is to serve God and His people. The rich man couldn't trust Jesus. He couldn't understand that giving away is really becoming spiritually rich.

In a similar vein, many centuries ago, the prophets of the Old Testament were preparing people to look at the holiness of God. Most prophets lived in unjust and exploitative communities in which the weak and vulnerable were subjected to all sorts of injustice and exploitation. Prophet Amos talked about it. He sided with the poor and fought for justice. He says, "Prepare to meet your God,"[30] turning away from sinful ways. Prophet Isaiah talked about light coming out of darkness. He urged people to get ready to witness the power of God. He went on to talk about the desert blossoming and the wolf and sheep lying down together in peace. Jeremiah lamented the evil deeds of people but he said that God was the potter and we are clay in His hands. Hosea cried that the Israelites had become like prostitutes and called them to turn to God. The message of the prophets, in a nutshell, was to repent, leave or mend your old ways and take on new ways of compassion and service. This is how they tried to prepare the people of their generation for the God who is Holy, and Perfect.

Nowadays it looks like people with no interest in God don't even realize what they are missing. It is time for us to re-learn that it is not materialism or popularity that makes us really rich but it is the knowledge of the presence of God in Christ with us that makes us rich in the deepest sense. There is nothing as enriching as the love of Christ for us. No worldly wealth or asset can match it in making our lives really fulfilling. The joy and peace that God pours into the hearts that seek Him is indescribable and it must be experienced to be understood. As one Indian hymn puts it, "It is sweeter than the sweetest honey." When we draw close to God we experience His love – an experience which is special and unique. Knowing that growing closer to God is the first step in our preparation for a life with him eternally cannot be overstated.

Habakkuk, the prophet says, "Though the fig tree does not bud and there are no grapes on the vines, though the olive crop fails and the fields produce no food, though there are no sheep in the pen and no cattle in the stalls, yet I will rejoice in the LORD, I will be joyful in God my Savior."[31] The joy of being with God cannot be put into words any better. The prophet amongst other biblical writers knew that if you have God, you have everything. On the other hand, if you have everything else and not God you really have nothing worth having. Making space for God in our lives and staying close to Him is the first step in our preparation.

Preparation is the way to excel

Peter once asked Jesus, look we have left everything and followed you. Jesus said, "Truly I tell you, there is no one who has left house or brothers or sisters or mother or father or children or fields, for my sake and for the sake of the good news, who will not receive a hundredfold now in this age—houses, brothers and sisters, mothers and children, and fields, with persecutions—and in the age to come eternal life."[32] So we learn that preparation, above all, is to delight in the presence of Jesus with us in this life and in this world itself. In other words, eternal life begins now. This is re-asserted in the Lord's Prayer when we pray – Thy kingdom come.

All that matters is you and I prepare. John the Baptist's central message was preparation. He came forth singing his message for the whole world to hear, "Repent and believe. Prepare the way of the Lord. Prepare to welcome God. Make the path straight for the Lord."

In our communities, we are proud of past glories, we are proud of how we got to where we are in our evolutionary thinking, civilization, culture and advances in science. We are proud of the advances in technology too. There is nothing wrong with learning our past or basking in past glory, but often we stop there. We need to look into the future too. Looking into the future deploying our imaginative power has to form part of the preparation. There is no substitute for preparation.

The significance of preparation – Two analogies

Analogies may help to understand how to go about the process of preparation. Suppose you get a letter from the Queen saying that she is coming to your home in two weeks' time and she wants to have lunch with you. Imagine you haven't had enough time to prepare. Eventually, the Queens arrives. To your embarrassment, the carpets are dirty and the living room doesn't look neat. Things are not in the right place in your home. How disconcerting it would be if the Queen arrives when you are not ready at all.

On the other hand, imagine the Queen has said that she is coming for lunch. You take time to prepare. New carpets are laid and beautiful paintings are fixed on the walls. Everything is sparkling clean. Things are spotless in your home. Hot food is ready and everything is in the right place. You get your best clothes on and you are confident and happy to welcome the Queen. What joy is that? The Queen arrives and enjoys lunch with you and is impressed. In fact, in this chapter, we are talking about preparing for the King of all kings, God Himself. The God who created everything and who gives us everything. We need to prepare for a life with Him. We are talking about preparing not our homes but our hearts. Preparation and being ready makes all the difference.

Another analogy pertains to a concert. Imagine the musicians haven't rehearsed. Songs are all over the place and you are dismayed with the disharmony amongst the musicians and singers. You can't wait for it to end. Imagine, on the other hand, the concert is held after many rehearsals. Then the songs and music are played in harmony. Preparation pays off. How joyful is that?

The fact is we are people who prepare. We spend years in school and college preparing for our future. As we grow into adults and step into the wider world whether we are single or building a family, we prepare our dream homes and lives. We prepare for retirement too. God-inspired life and preparation to meet God go hand in hand. Preparing ourselves to meet God is a life-long preparation.

Preparation is to go deeper into the mystery of God's love for us

Once I learned a valuable lesson while praying. I felt an invitation to continue to pray and go deeper into the love of God. To see the rare and majestic animals you need to go deeper and deeper into the forest. When we pray and pray, we go deeper and deep enough to be nearer to God. We should pray beyond just skimming the surface. You cannot pray alone – even when you prepare to pray, God begins to listen. God invites us to go deeper so that He can reveal Himself to us.

Our life is given to us by God, to prepare ourselves to meet God. The meaning for all other purposes should be found in the light of this ultimate purpose. Preparing for the kingdom is also the greatest mission of the church. As a Vicar I see my role as preparing myself to meet God setting an example to those around me. My role also includes helping others prepare to meet God with joy and blessed assurance.

In the parable of the ten bridesmaids,[33] those who were prepared and took oil along with their lamps went with the bridegroom to the wedding banquet. Like the wise bridesmaids, we need to be prepared and our lights should shine for Christ. I also believe that when our lamps are lit for Christ, even if the oil gets over, God will replenish it for us.

We are put in this world to prepare ourselves to be with God, in His direct presence, for eternity. If you want to go and live in a different country you get to know the language, interests, habits, culture and way of thinking of the people there. Imitating the love, kindness, justice, wisdom and faith of Christ is the best way to prepare. Above all, we need the grace of God. God is generous and offers His grace to those who hunger, thirst and ask for it.

Questions for reflection or discussion

1. How important do you think preparing to meet God in His heavenly home is?
2. How would our life be when we serve God?
3. What do you think the word repentance means? Do you think we have to repent again and again and turn back to godly ways?
4. What are the similarities and differences between preparing for a holiday and preparing for our heavenly home?
5. Do you think living for Jesus and preparing for our heavenly home is one and the same thing? If you are in a group, please discuss.
6. What are the different tools we have to go deeper into the love of God for us?

6.5 Created to choose God in Christ: Letting go and taking on

For God so loved the world that he gave his only Son, so that everyone who believes in him may not perish but may have eternal life.[34]

I know where I am going, do you?
(Billy Graham)

In the previous section we scrutinized the joy of preparation. In this final sub-chapter, we will see that the most important decision we will ever make in life is whether to choose God or not.

If we look around our communities, society and the world, the biggest problem we see is mortality. Everyone knows that life in this world, in this physical body is short. It is temporary. It is transient. From the moment a child is born the problem of mortality appears. All the credits people have in their banks, the degrees they have earned from famous universities, the talents, abilities and strengths people boast about will perish because we are mortal beings.

How does society tackle the problem of mortality? First the world thinks that the solution is life enhancement. For example, look at the improvements medical science is now capable of providing to humanity. Millions of pounds are spent in the medical field every year to enhance life. New medicines are invented constantly, new surgeries are experimented and new treatments are discovered and implemented. Most of the time they help people to live longer and healthier. Treatments which were unimaginable in the seventeenth and eighteenth centuries are possible today. We all benefit from it. Extending lives and longer living is one solution to mortality even though the problem is not fully solved.

Another way by which the world has responded to the problem of mortality is by increasing the speed of life. Life is short. So the antidote for mortality is to increase speed or so the argument goes. For example, tractors were invented to speed up farming. Cars, trains and airplanes were invented for speedy travel.

And yet another solution for mortality is more consumption in less time. Fridges to preserve food and pressure cookers are two examples. Further, online shopping which became more popular during the Covid-19 pandemic gives us instant, easy and continues access to the newest products in the market.

Along with all of this, the speed of communication has increased. Pigeons carried messages in the past. Also, messages were sent through bottles that floated on the ocean. But now telephone and electronic means of communication give immediate access in any part of the globe, be it near or far. The problem of mortality is pushed away to a future date but not overcome completely by these worldly solutions.

Despite the best human efforts to tackle it the problem of mortality is still very much there. It hasn't gone away. It follows human beings like a shadow.

Still, we are not left without hope. The problem of mortality can be solved by building relationships. Our relationship with God gives us the assurance that life doesn't end with the grave. It is our relationship with God that finally solves the problem of mortality. God promises life in all its fullness eternally for His people. God is faithful. He keeps his promises. As John says, "For God so loved the world that he gave his one and only Son, that whoever believes in him shall not perish but have eternal life."[35] We see God's love for us in Jesus. In Him, we have the assurance of permanent life. Our friendship with God's people will also continue in God's direct presence for ever literally. My prayer is that God will use you and me to make heaven crowded.

Choose God

A few years ago, one of my friends took me to a restaurant in London. He wanted me to taste different foods of different countries and so he took me to the place where it is served as a buffet. Whatever you eat the price is the same. I was excited to taste the different foods available in that restaurant and I was quite hungry too. So, I took bits and pieces from everywhere. In my overexcitement I ate delicacies from several countries. I overate and was immobilized. My stomach was so heavy that I felt I could have been content with only what I needed. Then I realized that gluttony was really a sin. We should be able to do without over doing things for fear of missing out.

A similar problem could happen to our intellectual life as well. Different philosophies prevail in our world. There are many ideologies about life and people. We take bits and pieces from everywhere. Different philosophies and doctrines eventually confuse people.

In this confusing and chaotic world, the biggest question for us to answer is this: Who is our Savior? God in Jesus is greater than any ideology or any philosophy. God sent a Savior – Jesus – as He promised. To Colossians, Paul writes, "Christ is the visible image of the invisible God."[36] (In other words, He is God himself.) He is one through whom all things were created and He is the head and the church is His body. In Him, the fullness of God was pleased to dwell. Paul's message was clear: Jesus the Christ is the supreme one. He is the Savior.

Similarly, for John, Jesus is not a philosophy or an ideology or a doctrine, but he is the Word made flesh. He is the light that shineth in darkness. He is the revelation of God's glory in its fullness. He is the truth. In fact, this is a profound transformation of the ordinary meaning of truth in John's time. John indicates that in Him the true, the authentic, the ultimate reality is present. Even early church had this problem. They often put doctrines and ideologies above humanity and God in Jesus, the Savior.

Who is your Savior? People around us in our communities and society look at everything to choose from. They ask if they should choose secularism or science as their Savior, or they should choose anything else. Should they choose money or fame or popularity or should they choose a celebrity or should they choose themselves as their own Savior. We need to choose wisely. Perhaps in our teenage years we think what is life all about? What is the truth? Who can really save us? Then we go to university/college or get into a job and some of us get a family thinking and anticipating we will find the truth there. But whatever we study or work, we come out with the old question. What is the truth?

The answer to that question depends on who our Savior is. Have we accepted the grace of God given to us in Jesus, on the cross and the resurrection? The cross achieved something the greatest powers, economies and ideologies of the world couldn't achieve, which is the re-establishment of our union with God now and eternally. The Bible puts it clearly that we need God's grace given to us in and through the cross of Christ. When we open our hearts, hands and lives to receive God's grace our lives change. We begin to store treasures in heaven. Accepting God in Christ as our Savior will shape how we spend our time and money, and what we want to commit to in life. It will shape our worship and prayer life.

John's message, in a nutshell, is that when we choose Jesus, we will meet him except in one form, a form in which we can't write down. But we may encounter him in one sentence of the Bible, or in one sentence in a hymn or in one sentence of a sermon or even in stillness. This sentence or stillness is not the truth but it may open us up for the truth. Suddenly, true reality may appear like the brightness of light in a formerly dark, muddled and confused place.

John, who wrote the gospel and his letters, has to say at the end that Jesus is the one who liberates us; He is the power of love, for God is love. This is to say that to choose Jesus as our Savior is to choose love – for Jesus is the embodiment of God's love.

Jesus left His heavenly citizenship and took our earthly citizenship so that we might be citizens of heaven. Our real citizenship depends on our Savior. Like in a buffet there is too much to choose from, in this world we have too much to choose from as well. We can't have everything. We have to choose wisely.

Jesus did conquer the world – through his cross and resurrection – and He promises to give us the grace to do the same. Humanity's greatest enemies are sin, guilt and death. God in Jesus gave himself on the cross so that we can be set free from sin and guilt. The cross teaches us that God's weakest point is much stronger than the world's strongest point. The resurrection of Jesus gives us the hope and assurance that when we put our trust in God in Christ and live differently even though we die, we will live. When we commit to live a God-filled life we receive the grace and courage to conquer the world and its value system. We receive the grace and courage not to give in to the trials and persecutions of this world. We also gain the grace to receive forgiveness for the past and the courage to rise above the temptations and the transient distractions of this world.

Jesus wasn't defeated but conquered the world because he transcended the pressures, the temptations, the distractions and the trivial glories of this world.

God who has brought you so far will help you get through – Trust God, Stick with God

The Old Testament concept called Ebenezer means thus far God has brought us. Samuel, the great prophet uses this word in I Samuel 7. We read an interesting story there. The Israelites were afraid of the Philistines because they were strong, brave and many in number. The Israelites were afraid. In fact, they were surrounded by the Philistines and so were terrified. Thus, they came together and told Samuel, the prophet, "Please pray for us." And Samuel built an altar and offered a burnt offering to God.

The Israelites chased the Philistines away. After these things happened Samuel placed a big stone, offered thanks to God and called that place Ebenezer. Ebenezer literally means God has brought us so far. God has brought you and me thus far too.

In our personal, social and spiritual lives God has brought us so far. The God who has brought us so far will guide us in the future too to live a God-inspired life if we wish to.

Jehovah Jireh

Another Old Testament concept is Jehovah Jireh[37] which means

God is the one who provides. When Abraham went with Isaac with an uncertain future, he found a ram. He said Jehovah Jireh – the Lord provides. God is working in the world and in us, quite beyond the limits of our budgets, plans, structures and expectations. His gospel lived out in faith and hope has the power to break beyond our timidity and insufficiency. He invites us to recognize who He is and to change into what we can be and become because He is the one who provides.

Letting go and taking on

There is an Indian story about a stray dog being chased by other stray dogs because it has a piece of bone in its mouth. After a long chase the dog lets go of the bone. The other dogs go for it but the dog that let go gives a big sigh of relief. It was truly free. It didn't have to rush and run anymore. In the same way, when we let go of our egos and burdens, we find relief and liberation.

We are made to be temples of God. When we are truly empty, we can ask God to make His home in us. We can be filled with God's power and love. We can commit to live a God-inspired life for the rest of our lives. We can then begin to experience glimpses of God, through faith, in our everyday ordinary life. In other words, eternal life can begin in this world now.

The truth is if we want to live a fulfilling life based on faith in God in Christ, we certainly need to let go of our own culture and learn the culture of Jesus cemented by the true inwardness of His teachings. He was in constant communion with God the Father through prayer. That was where He received His joy and strength. God's love for His people overflowed from Jesus to others in word and deed. He exemplified how we should love God and love one another. He is the model for us when it comes to seeking God's kingdom and His righteousness first. It is God's assurance to us that everything else will be given to us (perhaps in the form of a content heart) when we put Him first in our lives.

Our life is God-given; it is priceless and precious. It becomes worth living when our lives are filled with God and His joy in our hearts. It becomes worth living when we live a life inspired by God. Life sometimes can be challenging but the redeeming good news is that the love of Christ on the cross has the power to save the entire world. The whole of you and I must and will undergo a transformation through the love shown on the cross by Jesus Christ. We have to step back and ask God to take control. When that happens our priorities and attitudes change, God's ways for us are clarified – one step at a time – and we become fully alive. My faith is that when we put our trust in God, enjoy God and live a holy life as best as we can, even if we are thrown in "hell" for whatever reason, God in Christ will stay with us. Such is His love for us – so let us not be afraid but believe and live fully in peace, light, love and hope.

Questions for reflection or discussion

1. What do you think is the best solution for the problem of mortality?
2. What does it mean to say "choose God"?
3. In what ways has God been Ebenezer in your life?
4. Do you believe that God has already provided all that is needed for our salvation in Jesus?
5. How can we become more like Jesus?
6. How can we store treasures in heaven?
7. How will your life change if you seek God first? How will your life change if you commit to live a God-inspired life?

References

Chapter 1

1. Psalm 19. 1–6 NIV
2. Psalm 139.14 NRSV
3. John 1
4. Psalm 119. 175a NLT
5. John 15. 4–6 NIV
6. John 20. 21–22 NIV
7. Jeremiah 9. 23–24a NRSV
8. Deuteronomy 4. 29 NIV
9. Matthew 22. 35–38 NRSV
10. Romans 8. 38–39 NIV
11. Psalm 100.3 NIV
12. I John 4.4 NLT
13. Isaiah 43. 1 NLT
14. Psalm 24.1 NIV
15. Matthew 22 NLT
16. Max Lucado, The Applause of Heaven (Nashville: Thomas Nelson, 1996) 190
17. Deuteronomy 33.27a NIV
18. John 10. 28–29 NIV
19. Matthew 5. 1–12. A slightly different version can be found in Luke 6. 20–26
20. John 14. 1–2
21. John 17. 16 ESV
22. https://www.goodreads.com/quotes/32394-if-you-look-at-the-world-you-ll-be-distressed-if
23. https://www.cambridge.org/core/journals/journal-of-law-and-religion/article/happiness-and-the-restless-heart-an-augustinian-confession/B6E84F9D2ED5428ABB5B76598BA3FEAF
24. Proverbs 9.10a NIV

25. Psalm 95. 6 ESV
26. I Chronicles 16.29
27. Deuteronomy 10.20 NIV
28. Exodus 20. 3–5 and Deuteronomy 5.7
29. Matthew 4. 10 NIV
30. For instance, see Revelation 5. 1–14 and 19.1–8
31. Matthew 11.28 NIV
32. Timothy Radcliffe, *Why Go to Church?* (London: Continuum, 2008) 208
33. https://www.biographyonline.net/sport/athletics/eric-liddell.html

Chapter 2

1. https://www.theclearingnw.com/blog/spiritual-beings having-a-human-experience
2. https://www.theguardian.com/society/2018/jan/07/is everything-you-think-you-know-about-depression wrong johann-hari-lost-connections
3. Matthew 5: 23, 24 NIV
4. Mark 1: 16 NIV
5. For instance, see Mark 14: 24 or Matthew 26: 28
6. Ephesians 4. 3–6 NIV
7. https://www.theclearingnw.com/blog/spiritual-beings-having-a-human-experience
8. Ephesians 4. 11–13 NIV
9. Matthew 16. 26 ESV Also see, Mark 8.36
10. Mark 12.31 NRSV
11. Ephesians 1. 15 ff
12. For the whole story, read Luke 19. 1–10
13. See, Luke 10
14. See, Matthew 25. 40
15. http://krishnamurti.abundanthope.org/index_htm_files/The-New-Being-by-Paul-Tillich.pdf
16. I Samuel 16.7b NIV

17. https://www.goodreads.com/quotes/6826-people-are-like-stained-glass-windows-they-sparkle-and-shine-when
18. Acts 6
19. Acts 6
20. Isaiah 52. 7
21. Romans 10.15
22. Ephesians 1. 22–23 NRSV
23. http://anglicancompass.com/wp-content/uploads/2019/01/HolyOrdersTaskForce_Section-3_Principles-of-Anglican-Ecclesiology.pdf
24. John 17: 21 NIV (emphasis added)
25. Dietrich Bonhoeffer, The Cost of Discipleship (London: SCM Press, 1959), 219
26. I Cor 12: 12–26 NRSV
27. Romans 14: 19 NIV
28. Jeremiah 29.13 NIV
29. Acts 19: 8–10
30. For a detailed analysis see, "The Extraordinary Synod," (editorial) *Vidyajyothi* 49 (1985), p. 106.
31. http://www.vatican.va/roman_curia/pontifical_councils/interelg/documents/rc_pc_interelg_pro_20051996_en.html
32. *Guidelines on Dialogue* (Geneva: World Council of Churches, 1982), pp. iv.
33. Psalm 148: 7–13a NIV
34. Matthew 10: 29
35. Colossians 1: 17 NIV
36. Romans 8. 20–22. It is told that reflecting on this passage Martin Luther – looking at his dog – said, "And you will have a golden tail."
37. Psalm 8:5–8 NLT
38. For instance, see Genesis 1:26–30
39. Job 38:4 NRSV
40. Psalm 50. 10–12 NRSV
41. Psalm 89:11–12

42. Psalm 16:2, 8
43. Psalm 107:33–34
44. Hosea 14:4-7, 9

Chapter 3

1. Psalm 25. 4, 5 NIV
2. Micah 6. 8 NRSV
3. https://www.bbc.co.uk/radio4/news/anyquestions_transcripts_20080411.shtml
4. Romans 12. 1–2 NIV
5. Psalm 119. 105 NRSV
6. Psalm 127. 1–2 NRSV
7. 2 Thessalonians 3.10 NLT
8. See, Matthew 5. 13–16
9. Ephesians 2:10 NIV
10. Bamidele, Oby, *Purpose – lessons in life and living* (Essex: Wisegate Resources Ltd, 2016)
11. In a similar vein, Rick Warren in his popular book talks about SHAPE. It is worth asking what the shape God has made you is. S stands for Spiritual gifts, H stands for Heart, A stands for Abilities, P stands for Personality and E stands for Experiences. For details see, Warren, Rick, *The Purpose Driven Life: What on earth am I here for?* (Grand Rapids, Michigan: Zondervan, 2002) pp. 234-248. This insight is also covered in a course by CPAS. See, https://www.cpas.org.uk/advice-and-support/exploring-call/your-shape/#.XlUWvKj7TIV
12. John 15. 18, 19 NIV
13. John 17. 13b
14. Luke 10. 5,6 NIV
15. https://bible.org/illustration/violinist
16. See, Romans 4
17. Ecclesiastes1.9b NIV
18. II Timothy 2.3 NRSV

19. II Corinthians 11.24 NIV
20. http://bfmindia.blogspot.com/2021/01/revelation-for-liberation-by-rev-dr-t-p.html
21. Galatians 5. 19–20
22. Galatians 5. 22–23
23. Matthew 16. 24 NRSV
24. Luke 10. 25–37

Chapter 4

1. Isaiah 41.13 NIV
2. Romans 3. 23
3. Mark 10. 18b NIV
4. John 1
5. John 21
6. John 21: 17
7. 1 Chronicles 29:17 ESV
8. Matthew 13: 1–9, 18–23
9. Matthew 13: 24–30, 36–43
10. Micah 6. 8 NIV
11. Exodus 4
12. Judges 6: 14 NRSV
13. Mark 10. 35–45
14. Luke 10. 25–37
15. Matthew 25. 31–46
16. Luke 4. 18,19
17. https://henrinouwen.org/meditation/free-to-be-compassionate/
18. https://www.passiton.com/inspirational-quotes/7155-do-all-the-good-you-can-by-all-the-means-you
19. 1 Corinthians 9. 24 NIV
20. https://archangeloracle.com/2019/03/18/micah-divine-plan-2/
21. 2 Timothy 1: 14
22. James 2. 15–17 NRSV

23. Matthew 25:40 NIV
24. Author unknown
25. John 6. 37–39, NRSV
26. James 1. 13, 14 NIV
27. Proverbs 7. 25–26 NIV
28. 2 Peter 2. 9 NIV
29. Luke 22.40 NIV
30. John 15. 5
31. Jeremiah 29. 13–15 NRSV
32. James 4. 8a NRSV
33. Psalm 119. 2–3 NRSV

Chapter 5

1. 2 Corinthians 4. 8–9 ESV
2. https://www.treasurequotes.com/quotes/when-the-world-pushes-you-to-your-knees-your
3. I Corinthians 10.13 ESV
4. I Peter 1. 6b–7 NRSV
5. See, Job 2. 9
6. John 9. 3 NRSV
7. Yancey, Philip, *Amazing Grace* (Grand Rapids, Zondervan, 1997)
8. I Corinthians 10. 13 NIV
9. Isaiah 49. 13–16 NIV
10. http://www.knowjesus.com/Encourage.shtml
11. Matthew 28. 20 NRSV
12. Matthew 17. 16
13. https://poets.org/poem/ode-west-wind
14. John 14. 27 NRSV
15. Philippians 4. 7 NRSV
16. Psalm 34. 18 NRSV
17. https://www.goodreads.com/quotes/623193-we-can-ignore-even-pleasure-but-pain-insists-upon-being
18. I Peter 5. 7 NRSV

19. Matthew 11. 28
20. Isaiah 40. 31 NRSV
21. Galatians 5. 22–23
22. Psalm 139.NRSV
23. John 9. 3 NLT
24. https://www.goodreads.com/quotes/8311235-affiiction-makes-god-appear-to-be-absent-for-a-time
25. In II Timothy 4: 8 NRSV
26. See, Ephesians 4
27. Isaiah 40. 1 NRSV
28. Revelation 3. 20 ESV
29. Matthew 6. 25–34
30. Matthew 6. 26 ESV
31. Matthew 6:25 NRSV
32. Matthew 11. 28 NRSV
33. https://www.oneplace.com/ministries/daily-hope/read/devotionals/daily-hope-with-rick-warren/problems-force-us-to-depend-on-god-daily-hope-with-rick-warren-may-15-2018-11791573.html
34. Psalm 34. 18 NIV
35. Hebrews 12. 2 NIV
36. https://www.goodreads.com/quotes/32394-if-you-look-at-the-world-you-ll-be-distressed-if
37. https://www.goodreads.com/quotes/9210082-trailing-clouds-of-glory-do-we-come-from-god-who
38. For the full story see, 2 Kings 5. 20–22, 25–26
39. Matthew 6. 9–10, Luke 21.19
40. 2 Corinthians 4. 17–18

Chapter 6

1. John 15. 18, 19 NIV
2. John 14. 2,3 NIV
3. John 14.1–6
4. https://www.churchtimes.co.uk/articles/2020/9-april/

features/features/interview-with-john-polkinghorne-christ-
s-resurrection-and-ours

5. I Thessalonians 4. 13–18
6. Gooder, Paula, The Risen Existence (Norwich: Canterbury Press, 2009) 2
7. Exodus 14: 15 NRSV
8. Isaiah 26.2 NRSV
9. Romans 6
10. Romans 6.1ff
11. John 20.18 NRSV
12. Luke 24. 5 NIV
13. Luke 24.8
14. Acts 3: 14 NIV
15. John 20.20 NIV
16. Ecclesiastes 3.11b NLT
17. I Corinthians 15. 26
18. https://www.brainyquote.com/quotes/pierre_toilhard_de_chardi_160888
19. John 14, 2–3 NIV
20. Deuteronomy 26.15 ESV
21. https://preachitteachit.org/articles/detail/will-you-have-friends-in-heaven/
22. Rev 21. 11b NIV
23. Rev 21. 23 NIV
24. Rev 21. 4, 27
25. Psalm 16. 11 ESV
26. I Corinthians 13.12 NLT
27. Job 1. 21 NRSV
28. Psalm 103. 15–17 NRSV
29. See Matthew 19. 16-30
30. Amos 4.12c NIV
31. Habakkuk 3. 17, 18 NIV
32. Mark 10.29, 30 NRSV
33. Matthew 25.1–13

34. John 3.16 NRSV
35. John 3. 16 NIV
36. Colossians 1. 15a NLT
37. Genesis 22.14

CIRCLE
BOOKS

CHRISTIAN FAITH

Circle Books explores a wide range of disciplines within the field
of Christian faith and practice. It also draws on personal testimony
and new ways of finding and expressing God's presence in the
world today.
If you have enjoyed this book, why not tell other readers by
posting a review on your preferred book site. Recent bestsellers
from Circle Books are:

I Am With You (Paperback)
John Woolley
These words of divine encouragement were given to John Woolley
in his work as a hospital chaplain, and have since inspired and
uplifted tens of thousands, even changed their lives.
Paperback: 978-1-90381-699-8 ebook: 978-1-78099-485-7

God Calling
A. J. Russell
365 messages of encouragement channelled from Christ to two
anonymous "Listeners".
Hardcover: 978-1-905047-42-0 ebook: 978-1-78099-486-4

The Long Road to Heaven,
A Lent Course Based on the Film
Tim Heaton
This second Lent resource from the author of *The Naturalist and the Christ* explores Christian understandings of "salvation" in a five-part study based on the film *The Way*.
Paperback: 978-1-78279-274-1 ebook: 978-1-78279-273-4

Abide In My Love
More Divine Help for Today's Needs
John Woolley
The companion to *I Am With You*, *Abide In My Love* offers words of divine encouragement.
Paperback: 978-1-84694-276-1

From the Bottom of the Pond
The Forgotten Art of Experiencing God in the Depths of the Present Moment
Simon Small
From the Bottom of the Pond takes us into the depths of the present moment, to the only place where God can be found.
Paperback: 978-1-84694-066-8 ebook: 978-1-78099-207-5

God Is A Symbol Of Something True
Why You Don't Have to Choose Either a Literal Creator God or a Blind, Indifferent Universe
Jack Call
In this examination of modern spiritual dilemmas, Call offers the explanation that some of the most important elements of life are beyond our control: everything is fundamentally alright.
Paperback: 978-1-84694-244-0

The Scarlet Cord

Conversations With God's Chosen Women

Lindsay Hardin Freeman, Karen N. Canton

Voiceless wax figures no longer, twelve biblical women,
outspoken, independent, faithful, selfless risk-takers, come to life
in *The Scarlet Cord*.

Paperback: 978-1-84694-375-1

Will You Join in Our Crusade?

The Invitation of the Gospels Unlocked by the Inspiration of
Les Miserables

Steve Mann

Les Miserables' narrative is entwined with Bible study in this book
of 42 daily readings from the Gospels, perfect for Lent or anytime.

Paperback: 978-1-78279-384-7 ebook: 978-1-78279-383-0

A Quiet Mind

Uniting Body, Mind and Emotions in Christian Spirituality

Eva McIntyre

A practical guide to finding peace in the present moment that will
change your life, heal your wounds and bring you a quiet mind.

Paperback: 978-1-84694-507-6 ebook: 978-1-78099-005-7

Readers of ebooks can buy or view any of these bestsellers by
clicking on the live link in the title. Most titles are published in
paperback and as an ebook. Paperbacks are available in traditional
bookshops. Both print and ebook formats are available online.

Find more titles and sign up to our readers' newsletter at http://
www.johnhuntpublishing.com/christianity. Follow us on Facebook
at https://www.facebook.com/ChristianAlternative.